DISCONNECTED

How Six People from AT&T

Discovered the New Meaning of Work

in a Downsized Corporate America

BARBARA RUDOLPH

THE FREE PRESS

New York London Toronto Sydney Singapore

THE FREE PRESS
A Division of Simon & Schuster Inc.
1230 Avenue of the Americas
New York, NY 10020

THE FREE PRESS and colophon are trademarks
of Simon & Schuster Inc.

Designed by Carla Bolte

Manufactured in the United States of America

10   9   8   7   6   5   4   3   2   1

Library of Congress-Cataloging-in-Publication Data

Rudolph, Barbara, 1956–
    Disconnected : how six people from AT&T discovered the new meaning
of work in a downsized corporate America / Barbara Rudolph.
        p.   cm.
    Includes bibliographical references and index.
    ISBN 0-684-84266-1
    1. Employees—United States—Dismissal of—Case studies.
2. American Telephone and Telegraph Company.   3. Downsizing of
organizations—United States—Case studies.   4. Corporate culture—
United States—Case studies.   I. Title.
HF5549.5.D55R83   1998
331.13'7813846'0973—dc21   97-46187
                                                                        CIP

*Lines from "Vacillation," by W. B. Yeats, reprinted with the permission of Simon & Schuster from
THE COLLECTED WORKS OF W. B. YEATS, Volume 1: THE POEMS, Revised and edited
by Richard Finneran. Copyright 1933 by Macmillan Publishing Company; copyright renewed © 1961
by Bertha Georgie Yeats.*

In memory of my father

CONTENTS

PREFACE

When I set out to find the protagonists for this book, I did not look for a representative sample of the population, whatever that might be. My approach was instinctively more journalistic than academic. I was searching for compelling life stories, and the ones I chose were those I believed would tell themselves.

Here, then, are six American men and women. They are not heroes or victims, symbols or spokesmen. I selected them not because they proved a theory or confirmed any personal preconceptions, but because I was drawn to them—in different ways and for different reasons.

All of them worked at AT&T and lost their jobs during the company's downsizings of the mid-1990s. Each of them made a journey from the old world of work to the new one—a transition all of us must navigate in corporate America. This journey is the subject of my book.

Their histories and characters are uniquely their own, and yet these six people share something precious. They have come to comprehend their value, independent of their corporate identity. They have claimed their personal dignity.

1 OVERVIEW

The world of work has changed.

In the following pages I chart the course of this change as it has unfolded in the lives of six people in corporate America. Downsized from AT&T, these men and women walked away from the old working world of loyalty, security, and community toward a new American workplace defined by blunt individualism and emotional detachment, and by a restless energy and mobility that can be both inspiring and daunting. "I must manage my own career" is the credo of the new company man.

As they negotiated this transition, these six people felt—intensely, privately, and sometimes painfully—the fundamental connection between work and sense of self, between who we are and what we do. This peculiarly American link between work and identity dates back to Puritanism: the Yankee interpretation of the Calvinist link between work and virtue, between honest labor and a man's salvation. That heritage endures. In Chicago or San Jose, one stranger may ask another "What do you do?" by way of a greeting, but one is much less likely to hear this phrase in Paris, Dublin, or Hong Kong.

For these six people, as for all Americans, work is a critical determinant of social and economic status. For many Americans—certainly those in the middle class—it is an important source of personal dignity. Unlike their working-class counterparts, middle-income Americans have had a reasonable expectation that their work would give them something more than money: a sense of purpose, a feeling of autonomy.

Today, that expectation only survives as a fragile hope. And the demise of white-collar job security (which has been the cornerstone of the American workplace since the end of World War II) has brought about a critical shift in our collective understanding of the role of work in our lives.

Middle-class job security began to erode in the late 1980s, when a wave of white-collar layoffs began. The prototypical victim was the fifty-year-old neighbor down the street who, to everyone's surprise, lost his job after fifteen years with the company. He wasn't fired, exactly; his position was eliminated in a reorganization. College-educated white-collar workers, most of them men, were especially stung by the force of these layoffs. Still, it was not until the presidential campaign in the winter of 1996 that the dimensions of this change were fully appreciated by middle-class Americans, resulting in a national debate about downsizing and job insecurity.

THE HISTORY OF JOB SECURITY

We start you in a Chevrolet, and we bury you in a Cadillac. (General Motors executive, circa 1960)

What we think of as "job security" had a relatively brief tenure in American history. It was one component of a uniquely halcyon chapter in U.S. economic development that began at the end of World War II and ended around the time of the first OPEC oil shock in 1973. During this postwar boom, the gross national product (GNP), productivity, and median family income were all on the rise.

For the first three decades of the century, as historian Sanford Jacoby recounts in *Employing Bureaucracy*, the average U.S. worker knew that he would be laid off at least once during the year. But by the late 1930s, the newfound strength of labor unions (by 1940, one in three manufacturing workers belonged to a union) and government pressure in the midst of the Great Depression gave birth to corporate paternalism. One result was that between 1935 and 1940, the number of workers covered by pension and health insurance plans soared.

At the core of the emerging new workplace was a social contract between employer and employee—in its purest form, an exchange of loyalty for security. This unwritten pact assumed a long-term attachment between worker and employer. It also had the critical effect of insulating workers from fluctuations in the economy that affected the value of their labor in the outside market.

The organization, meanwhile, acquired a stable and experienced pool of labor. Companies could exploit their employees' firm-specific knowledge—the awareness of a particular organization's strengths, quirks, and culture that only comes with time. Moreover, by this exchange of loyalty for security, the corporation was able to harness the very spirit of its workers, that special commitment which can be given freely but never bought.

As the postwar workplace evolved, the largest U.S. companies offered the most stable jobs. Even in the 1950s and 1960s, though, when the names of mighty American corporations like General Motors, Sears, Roebuck, and United States Steel had such resonance, they employed only a small fraction of the workforce. In 1965, for example, only 16 percent of all workers (11.3 million people) were employed by Fortune 500 firms. (The ratio of 16 percent still held in 1979, when the Fortune 500 payrolls reached 16.2 million, as it did in 1996, when 20.4 million of 134 million Americans worked for Fortune 500 companies.) Yet these corporations had a presence in the workplace that transcended their number of employees. They were the public face of American business, symbols of postwar prosperity; to many smaller firms (and their workers), they represented the ideal employer.

Their stature reflected the fact that the U.S. economy of the 1950s and 1960s was far more cohesive than it is today. A handful of brand-name firms within a few key sectors—most notably manufacturing and transportation—struck the dominant chords. It was a world of three television networks and one phone company, a single computer giant, and a small clique of regulated airlines.

By 1980, however, the postwar American economy had been transformed. A relatively simple structure had become complicated and diffuse. The service sector was exploding, technology was flourishing, and manufacturing had receded into the shadows. The U.S. economy inevitably became more differentiated—and more closely linked to a global market.

Shared Sensibility

The postwar workplace inspired and sustained a particular sensibility in the men and women who filled its cubicles and corner offices. It was shaped by the experience of a class and a generation: the college-educated, white-collar, middle-class baby boomers.

This sensibility was defined by a shared expectation of *what work means*—shared notions of the connection between work and personal identity. In describing this sensibility one uses words, like *dignity* and *fraternity*, that are now almost unthinkable in a corporate context. Job security made these feelings possible, because it gave people a sense of control over their working lives. Safety allowed them to aspire to loftier ideals, to some larger meaning and purpose in their jobs.

The workplace itself seemed predictable and manageable. Employees knew that if they respected the conventions of the corporate organization, they could master its hierarchy through talent and sheer perseverance. Was this world governed by fair play and selflessness? Of course not; the free market has always obeyed a rough sort of justice. But this environment encouraged a fundamental faith that one could shape and control the course of one's working life.

People approached their careers as a ladder to be climbed. Jobs were clearly defined, and paths of advancement plainly marked. Work histories followed a linear narrative line. Company men of the baby-boom generation did not need to spend thirty years at one firm, like their fathers. For William Whyte's organization men, who came of age in the Great Depression and valued security above all else, the totems of corporate distinction—the country club memberships, the plaques of appreciation (more ornate with each passing decade), the heavy gold watches of retirement—were respected as legitimate status symbols, and with a pristine faith that their children could never share. Yet these sons and daughters joined their own corporate organizations with a similar basic expectation: if they wanted to burrow into the bureaucracy, and stay for decades, they believed that they could. They could choose to follow their fathers' course even if they ultimately decided to reject it. This choice was a powerful freedom.

The baby boomers went to work in good faith. But while their fathers had happily submerged themselves in the organization as "team play-ers," the baby boomers thought of themselves as individualists. Whereas their fathers had idealized the corporation, their perspective was more skeptical. This was in keeping with the tenor of the 1960s, of course, when "big business" was a popular target. In 1967, *The Graduate's* fa-mous line, "I just want to say one word to you, just one word . . . plas-tics," became part of the national dialogue; that same year, thousands of demonstrators assailed Dow Chemical's management as hateful "baby killers." Still, among the men and (occasionally) women who made their living within the corporate structure, the firm was generally seen as a benign force.

For the growing ranks of the professional middle class—lawyers, en-gineers, and doctors, as well as company men (a group defined less by its financial status than by its college education)—the old workplace of-fered the possibility of real autonomy. These men and women could as-pire to not merely jobs but careers, even if they did not always find them. They could invest themselves in their work and hope to find some meaning in their labor.

Company men and women were loyal. The emotion was born of a sense of belonging to a larger community. Employees felt a personal identification with the organization; they believed that they shared the same fate. This sense of citizenship encouraged them to serve the long-term interest of the organization. Without it, the company man, in whatever incarnation, would not exist.

Where did this visceral faith come from? For many it was a family heritage. It is easy now to forget how commonplace it was to meet sec-ond-and third-generation employees at companies such as Eastman

Kodak, IBM, and especially AT&T (where many can still be found). The family legacy took root, reinforced by decades of easy prosperity, as the memory of the Depression faded.

The company was personified. A prevailing metaphor became a cliché, but it was grounded in a perceived truth: the company was a family. People trusted the organization, which is why so many could ultimately feel betrayed. Old-fashioned, unreconstructed employee loyalty was essentially a kind of love.

As the life stories that follow will affirm, people unconsciously repeat their own family dynamics, assume old roles, and act out old patterns of conflict in any organization. This behavior is inevitable in the workplace, the most important social environment outside the home. During the heyday of the "good" corporation, the identification was particularly intense. The company *was* family for many of its employees.

Loyalty could often take the form of unquestioned obedience to an impersonal, omnipotent bureaucracy. Managers could not refuse a transfer. Even the most absurd, unreasonable privileges of rank were respected. Freethinkers and whistle-blowers met with deep suspicion. The essential goodness of the corporation was never called into question.

Creative Destruction

Capitalism is by nature a form of change and never is, never can be, stationary.
(Joseph Schumpeter)

A confluence of changes, both inside and outside the firm, caused the old corporate structure and sensibility to come undone. Global competition and the rise of new technologies in the 1970s and early 1980s forced companies to reconceive their operations. To bolster profits, they needed to cut costs, and reducing payroll expenses—in other words, firing people—was an obvious place to start. As U.S. manufacturing came under global siege, the recession of the early 1980s sparked widespread layoffs of factory workers. Eventually, though, American industry became much more productive and competitive—producing more with fewer hands.

Layoffs of white-collar workers followed about a decade later, in the late 1980s. The rise of the service economy meant that many more Americans worked in white-collar jobs, so by definition that group was more vulnerable to downsizing. It had become clear, too, that as the ranks of middle managers had swelled in the 1970s and 1980s, many companies had become overstaffed.

Another factor was the rise of "investor capitalism," as Michael Useem has described the far-reaching influence of institutional shareholders, including mutual funds and retirement plans held by millions of American households. These stockholders cajoled and compelled companies to restructure, to downsize—to do anything to drive the stock price up. As executive compensation was increasingly tied to a company's stock performance (with CEO paychecks reaching historic and often outrageous levels during the 1990s bull market), investor capitalism became increasingly entrenched. Still more white-collar downsizing was often a crude form of mob psychology, as CEOs made the fashion of "re-engineering" synonymous with systemic layoffs.

All this downsizing was part of a deep transformation of the workplace. Rapid changes in technologies, shorter product cycles, and relentless competitive pressures meant that companies had to reinvent themselves continually. This almost perpetual state of flux necessarily diminished the storehouse of firm-specific knowledge that long job tenure had provided.

Most importantly, these changes intensified the demand for flexibility (a word that has become a staple of management guides) from both employers and workers. This flexibility appears most vividly in so-called contingent or alternate work relationships, in which an employee works for a company as an independent contractor, a part-timer, or through a temporary agency. Though there is a debate about how best to define this sector of the labor pool, there is no doubt that the category is rapidly expanding. The prevalence of outsourcing is another illustration, as more and more companies limit their ranks of permanent workers, by hiring outside firms to take over not only clerical work but financial, information technology, and human resources functions as well.

For many men and women trying to make their way in an organization, the word *flexibility* masks a corrosive uncertainty. In a world of constant flux, one never quite stands on solid ground.

Detachment and Disjunctions

Today, as they confront these changes, people are reassessing their notions of what work means. Yet old hopes still linger. In the voices of today's company men and women one hears a wistfulness, a tension between fading expectations and sharpening reality.

Compared with their baby-boom predecessors, Americans presently in their twenties and early thirties, members of Generations X and Y, have come of age with toughened expectations of what any corporate organization can provide. They generally expect to change jobs—and careers—more frequently than their older siblings and parents.

From both older and younger workers, then, there echoes the hopeful refrain of the flexible worker: "I must manage my own career." But what does this really mean, and who is most likely to achieve it? Fraternity is fleeting. For many, the sense of a collective purpose has been overtaken by individualism, and any surviving loyalty must be qualified. The emotional bond between a worker and an employer in this new environment becomes entirely conditional, and to speak of loyalty or trust in this context now becomes absurd.

Who will flourish in this new environment? People who can be not only flexible but also emotionally detached. They neither want nor expect the organization to act as their family manqué. As the organization lurches about, they will instinctively find their equilibrium: They won't take corporate changes and disruptions personally. And they certainly won't take them to heart.

In this context, restlessness will prove to be an asset. This is an environment in which people constantly look over their shoulders, ready to jump at a moment's notice to another department, another project, or another company.

Some workers will find freedom in this motion, enjoying the challenge of the chase. In *White Collar Blues*, Charles Heckscher describes the emergence of a new professional loyalty, in which people make a "commitment to a mission or task rather than to a company." They engage in an enterprise for a prescribed period of time, then move on.

The trick in all this is timing. Finding the next mission or project as soon as the present one ends is no simple task. Here the laws of the market will prevail, and those employees whose skills and talents are in demand will have the edge. Now employers have little incentive to teach their workers the skills they will need in the open market. How can a company justify such an investment when both the worker and the employee feel only a contingent connection to each other?

In the wake of dislocation and shared uncertainty, class boundaries blur. If middle-class workers have lost so much of their job security and feel such an attenuated sense of purpose in their work, how can they distinguish themselves from the working class? They can no longer assume, as they once did, that they work for something more than a wage. It was this expectation, more than the obvious gulf between physical and mental labor, that once set them apart from the working class.

Even so, there can be no question that class issues are very much with us. In fact, they form an interesting subtext to the economic debate about downsizing.

SOFT STATISTICS

By the mid-1990s, after American workers had endured years of white-collar layoffs, it seemed as though only one of two opposing scenarios could be true: Either we had traveled overnight from a world of absolute job security to a Hobbesian struggle in which no one's livelihood was safe, or nothing had changed at all.

The statistics support neither extreme. There is no evidence, for example, of what economists call a secular shift—an increase in the average job loss rate for the 130 million working Americans. (The government's overall job displacement rate, which tracks the percentage of workers who lose their jobs, stood at 3.2 percent for 1993–94 versus 3.1 percent in 1985–86, a comparable point in the business cycle.) Dramatic economic change that affects an entire population is always rare. In his classic text, *Principles of Economics*, Alfred Marshall expressed that truth in the old axiom, *Natura non saltus facit* ("Nature makes no leaps").

The data do offer compelling evidence of an erosion in job security between the 1980s and 1990s for white-collar Americans. It is most vivid for college-educated men, who represent about 15 percent of the workforce. The statistics signal a major shift in the life of a class and a related change in our collective understanding of the meaning of work.

Of course, the white-collar worker with a college degree is still much better off than a younger, less educated blue-collar worker. But the traditional armor provided by work experience and a college education has been seriously tarnished.

As the Department of Labor's Displaced Workers Survey (DWS) testifies, 7.3 percent of all blue-collar workers with three or more years on the job (employees who would be expected to enjoy some security) lost their jobs in the recession of 1981–82. For the same time period a decade later (1991–92), that percentage had fallen to 5.2 percent, and for the next two years (1993–94) it was down to 4.2 percent. During the same decade, white-collar layoff rates rose dramatically—from 2.6 percent in 1981–82 to 3.6 percent in 1991–92 before falling to 3.2 percent during the 1993–94 period.

Yet although this survey is the most important source of data for any economic analysis of job security, few people outside academia appreciate how fragile its numbers are. A brief explanation will suffice.

The survey, which appears as a biennial supplement to the Census Bureau's monthly Current Population Survey, has been conducted every two years since 1984. It draws on a sample of 50,000 U.S. households, and different people are interviewed for each report. Researchers ask this question: "During the last three calendar years, did you lose or leave your job because your plant or company closed or moved, your position or shift was abolished, there was insufficient work, or another similar reason?" If the answer is yes, interviewers turn to a list of follow-up questions that more narrowly define the lost job, its industry and occupation categories, and its wages and benefits.

Every four years, though, the DWS addresses the more slippery subject of job tenure. There is one question: "How long have you been with your current employer?" There are no follow-up questions to determine *why* a person changed jobs. Was he laid off, or did he quit? The statistics cannot say.

The job-tenure debate becomes especially convoluted because the Labor Department decided to rewrite the survey question in 1983. Where census takers had previously asked, "How long have you been in your current *job?*" after 1983 they asked, "How long have you been with your current *employer?*"

"It's a huge break in the series. We just don't know what we were getting before 1983," says Jay Meisenheimer, an economist at the Bureau of Labor Statistics whose job it is to pore over the job-tenure data. As a result, it is impossible to compare this data accurately between the early 1980s and the 1990s.

Almost certainly, the pre-1983 survey question effectively understated job tenure. Imagine that a person worked as a computer programmer for the XYZ Corporation and then took a job as a systems manager for the same company. In 1980, the Department of Labor would have recorded that person as someone who had changed jobs, even though he was working for the same firm throughout the period. After 1983, though, such a scenario would not be categorized as a change, and the worker's reported job tenure would consequently be longer.

Since the data does not identify why a person changed jobs, one cannot simply equate short job tenure with job insecurity: a person who willingly changes jobs may very well act out of confidence that a new and better job is waiting. Still, on the whole, long tenure is reasonably viewed as a general indicator of job stability, because it means that a person has the choice of remaining with the same employer. For many Americans, however, this option no longer exists.

Finally, the Displaced Workers Survey is handicapped by the fact that the government only collects information on one job loss for each individual interviewed. Two layoffs or ten layoffs: the government survey would record the answer as one job loss. This is a significant limitation. "Since it is possible (and not rare) for workers to have lost more than one job in a five-year (or three-year) period," notes Princeton economist Henry Farber, "the DWS cannot be used to measure the total quantity of job loss."

———————

Economists can consult another set of statistics to study job security—the Panel Survey of Income Dynamics (PSID), conducted by the University of Michigan's Institute of Social Research—but it has a different set of flaws. Its chief virtue is that it tracks the same people over an extended period of time (the DWS, as noted above, interviews different respondents for each of its reports). Since 1967, PSID researchers have tracked 5,000 households, or about 17,000 individuals, following the children as they leave home.

In its early years, though, the PSID survey confined itself to interviewing heads of households; the exclusion of married working women until 1980 is an obvious and important limitation. Another major shortcoming is that the PSID data fail to separate voluntary and involuntary job changes. Finally, the PSID sample is quite small (5,000 families, versus 50,000 households for DWS).

For these reasons, the DWS data, however imperfect, provide the more reliable information on job security.

JOB TENURE

The sensibility of the new workplace is defined by contingency, but is that feeling grounded in fact? Is stable, long-term employment actually disappearing from American business? The government's controversial job tenure data are central to this debate.

Those who argue that nothing much has changed in the American workplace point out that the overall median job tenure remains constant at four years; that 30 percent of American workers can claim ten or more years of job tenure; and that the average American can still expect to work at eight or ten different jobs before he or she retires. These facts have not changed for decades.

These averages, though, are misleading, because they trail the trend. Many fifty-year-olds are hanging on as longtime company men, propping up the job-tenure median—but not for much longer.

In fact, the data clearly reveal that middle-aged men, who came of age with the greatest expectations of job stability and who still represent the dominant face of American business, know their chances of becoming company veterans have dramatically declined.

The overall median job tenure may have remained constant at four years, but it has declined significantly for middle-aged men. The Displaced Workers Survey reports that between 1983 and 1996, median job tenure for men aged 35 to 44 fell from 7.3 to 6.1 years; for men aged 45 to 54, it dropped from 12.8 to 10.1 years. Statistically, these are very substantial declines.

In the universe of workers with ten or more years of tenure, one sees the same pattern: no change in the aggregate, but a marked change for middle-aged men. Overall, about 30 percent of all workers claimed ten or more years of tenure in 1996, a figure that has fluctuated only slightly since 1983. For men between the ages of 40 and 44, however, it dropped from 51.1 percent in 1983 to 41.7 percent in 1996; for ages 45 to 49, it fell from 57.8 percent to 50.8 percent; and for men aged 50 to 54, it fell from 62.3 percent to 54.9 percent. Even if one takes into account the fact that some of these men chose to change jobs, many of them surely did not. This group has good reason to feel vulnerable.

Interestingly, women's tenure averages have been moving in the opposite direction. In 1983, for example, among women aged 40 to 44, only 23.4 percent claimed ten or more years' job tenure; this figure increased to 30.4 percent by 1996. In the early 1980s, there were fewer women who had been steadily working for the previous decade, so by definition fewer women could have worked in one job for ten years. By the 1990s, because more women were employed (and fewer of them left their jobs when they married or had children), female job tenure medians began to rise.

This is not to say, however. that women feel protected from the threat of job insecurity. Far from it. As they look at the thinning ranks of veteran company men, they see their own future reflected.

AT&T

The tensions and strains of the changing workplace have appeared in bold relief at AT&T. An icon of American industrialism, AT&T in recent years has been a deeply troubled company, but it is still a force to be reckoned with in the new information age. Because of the Bell System's singular history as a regulated monopoly where lifetime employment was the expectation of its white collar (though never its factory) workers, we have seen at AT&T the starkest contrast between the old and the new working world. Very few companies offered such unshakable job security or inspired such deep loyalty.

AT&T's corporate culture in this period has been an uneasy blend of fading group loyalty and a new, aggressive individualism. The company must reconcile its heritage as a paternalistic pillar of corporate America and its role as one of many firms vying to dominate the intensely competitive telecommunications business, where technologies are rapidly changing.

Back when AT&T was still Ma Bell—not so very long ago—employees came to work for the rest of their lives. Even as late as 1996, the majority of AT&T employees had been with the company for at least fifteen years—dating back to a time when the Bell System was whole and downsizing had not yet begun.

AT&T had a clear and compelling mission (universal telephone service at an affordable price), and it infused in its employees a belief that they served an honorable cause. Then waves of layoffs and restructurings slashed about 120,000 jobs from AT&T between the 1984 breakup of the Bell System and 1995. (In that year, the company payroll totaled a little more than 300,000.) Still, the old connection between employer and employee—the implied exchange of devotion for security—had not been completely destroyed by the mid-1990s. Old-fashioned, unreconstructed loyalty was badly shaken, but something did survive.

PERSONAL PASSAGES

When they were cut loose from the corporate fold, the six people featured in this book—Vince Smith, Barbara David, Larry Nagel, Maggie

Starley, Kyle Stevens, and Tom Chase—had to navigate an arduous passage from the old to the new working world. (Kyle Stevens is the only pseudonym.) Though they represent a wide spectrum of circumstance and character, each lost a job and struggled to reclaim a sense of self in the wake of that loss. Each person had to rework his or her own calculus between work and identity.

Now middle-aged, these men and women first entered the workforce with typical expectations for their generation and their class. They hoped to find some modicum of security and satisfaction in their professional lives. (Maggie, a displaced telephone operator, is an exception; she kept a working-class sensibility even when she had a middle-class paycheck). For all six men and women, the minimalist aspirations of Generation X could not seem more remote.

Like many of their peers, these six came to see the organization as a kind of family. If they did not perceive it as benevolent, they assumed that it was more or less benign. They imbued it, too, with a rationality and coherence that did not actually exist. They lost sight of the fact that a company is not a purposeful entity but merely a set of shifting alliances that mix people and power, ego and intellect.

Downsizing reduced these men and women to names on a list, numbers on a spreadsheet. In the language of the bureaucracy, these people toiled in the vast middle, in neither the top nor the bottom 10 percent of all performers. Some found new jobs in a few months (outplacement agencies have found the national average is about three months), while others went without full-time work for more than a year.

These six individuals made personal choices and confronted their own particular fates. Yet in their stories, we can see common patterns of this human experience.

Resiliency and vulnerability shape the arc of this voyage. Inevitably, there are echoes of family history and patterns of behavior unconsciously repeated, in ways both affirming and self-defeating. Some were able to integrate this experience with remarkable grace, while others were nearly destroyed.

Moving On

Barbara David was a sales account executive; Larry Nagel, a Bell Labs engineer; and Vince Smith, a customer service manager. They each moved on to new firms—all of them, interestingly, much smaller than AT&T—and wrote second acts in their lives as company men and women.

Barbara relied upon an innate self-sufficiency born of a difficult life. Her identity as a capable businesswoman was always a critical part of her sense of self. That could not, and did not, change. Barbara knew that she would have to do what she had always done in the face of a deep loss: keep moving.

The downsizing intensified Barbara's sense that corporate environments are in flux everywhere. She believes that she now works for a company that is "kinder" than AT&T, but she also knows this appearance could easily change. Contingency, she now feels, is the only true connection between an organization and its employees.

Larry drew upon reserves of strength formed when he gained early fame by writing a widely used software program. After he received his Ph.D. from Berkeley in the early 1970s, Larry came to work at Bell Labs expecting to stay there for the rest of his professional life. But now he appreciates that along with that secure status came stagnation. He is now more engaged in his work at a small electronics company, and in this way has recaptured an important part of his identity.

Vince survived General Motors' downsizing in the early 1980s, but lost his job at AT&T in 1994 and endured more than a year of unemployment. Witnessing that first layoff had been a loss of innocence: GM had been his father's company, and for Vince a second home. The downsizing from AT&T was painful, therefore, but at least partially familiar.

Vince, an eldest son, found solace and strength in the legacy of his father's extraordinary life. While he once imagined that his career would unfold in a linear progression, he now sees himself "riding the waves." Conscientious by nature, Vince still feels obliged to "put in an honest day's work for a day's pay," but he does not expect to find personal validation in his job. Vince has all but severed the connection between his sense of himself as a worker and as a man.

A Return to the Fold

Maggie Starley was a telephone operator whose job was made obsolete by technology. Kyle Stevens was a business strategist who found himself in the wrong department when the downsizing dirge began. After months of being off the payroll, both reappeared at outposts of the old empire—Maggie at an AT&T customer care center, and Kyle at NCR (formerly the Global Information Solutions division of AT&T). Sobered and chastened, they had come back to the fold.

Maggie, a longtime union activist, had harbored no sentimental attachment to AT&T for any of the twenty-two years she worked for the company. Like many operators, though, she had taken pride in her work, believing that she provided a meaningful service. Her new job as a customer service representative uses more of her intelligence, but the work is also more anonymous and in some ways more alienating. Maggie hopes to recapture the sense of competence that she enjoyed as an operator. Most of all, though, she hopes to hang on to her new job for the next six years, when she will qualify for a full pension.

Kyle Stevens, the son of a thirty-year Navy veteran, never intended to become a company's loyal foot soldier, but slowly he did. After the downsizing, he tossed his old-fashioned loyalty like a pair of worn-out shoes and embraced an openly self-interested individualism. For Kyle, any tie to any organization must answer a simple question: What's in it for me? He subscribes to the vision of Charles Handy, the influential business theorist who argues that traditional jobs and career paths have become obsolete. The new organization, Handy has written, will consist of a small core of permanent employees surrounded by contingent workers. Living proof of this theory, Kyle has since returned to AT&T as an independent contractor.

Solitary Retreat

Tom Chase, a man of great intelligence and untouched potential, drifted through much of his life. He was far too creative to thrive in a bureaucracy like that of AT&T, but he lingered there for fifteen years.

When he lost his job, his life unraveled, and he found himself unable to move. This painful paralysis has now lasted for more than two years. For anyone who loves life—and Tom does—there is always hope. One morning he may take that first step and make a place for himself in the world. He will never again be a company man.

2 FATHER AND SON: CONTINUUM

Vincent Smith

For many men, the connection between work and identity is inextricably linked to the father-son relationship. Certainly that is the case for Vince Smith. Vince struggled for many years to bear the weight of his father's extraordinary legacy only to find, at a critical moment, that it was the very thing which gave him the strength to carry on.

At six feet and six inches tall, Vincent Smith moves with a stately, almost regal bearing. His shoulders squared and spine erect, he takes measured, deliberate strides. Neat almost to the point of fastidiousness, he has a formal air even when dressed in khaki shorts and a white polo shirt on a steamy summer's day. There is a courtliness about him, an old-fashioned solicitousness as he stoops, ever so slightly, to hear what someone has to say.

His face is dominated by a strong jaw and aquiline nose; his dark brown eyes are deep-set. An African-American man of quiet dignity, Vince is incapable of the aggressive self-promotion that governs so much of the corporate world. "I won't run from a fight," he says, "but boy, you'll never see me start one."

Beneath the unassuming demeanor, however, there lies an inner strength. Though he has attained neither great professional status nor fame, as his remarkable father did before him, Vince has one possession that he holds dear. "I will leave my children with a good and honorable name," he says. It is his father's name, and Vince Smith is his father's son.

When Vince was laid off from his job as an assistant staff manager during AT&T's 1994 downsizing, he endured sixteen months of unemployment before becoming a benefits manager for a health insurance company. During that time, Vince grappled to rediscover his personal identity in the wake of his professional loss. He reminded himself that he was not only a husband but the father of a twenty-year-old daughter and a sixteen-year-old son. Without a job I am still a man, he thought to himself, but what kind of a man? For Vince the answer had everything to do with his father, whose example he had sought to follow since he was a young boy.

Vince had been unemployed for three months when his father died of prostate cancer. Making the rounds of resumé-writing workshops and personnel interviews, Vince was both grieving his loss and seeking solace and guidance in the legacy of his father's life. "I felt driven to emerge from the layoff with the same dignity that my father showed as he lived and as he died."

Otis Smith was one of the Tuskegee airmen, the famous black U.S. Air Force regiment in World War II. After growing up poor in the segregated Memphis of the 1930s, Otis went on to college and law school when the war ended. By 1960, when he was thirty-eight years old, Smith had been the first black appointee to every job he held: the first black chairman of the Michigan Public Service Commission, the first black state supreme court justice in Michigan (and only the second black in any state to rise to that level), and, most dramatically, GM's first black general counsel when he claimed that chair in 1977.

Otis Smith was, above all, an honorable man. His eldest son, Vince, would become his loyal standard bearer.

"Vince was a gentleman even as a boy," recalls his uncle, Hamilton Smith. Three younger brothers were born in the space of five years, and Vince took seriously his father's frequent exhortations to set a good example. The four boys would all grow into tall men—as children, they looked like descending stair steps, people would say—and it seemed appropriate that when all of them were fully grown, Vince was still several inches taller than each of his brothers.

"He could rule with an iron hand," recalls Raymond, the next in line. Steven, the youngest of the clan, remembers childhood war games as an amusing case in point: "The pecking order held. I'd shoot Vince with my invisible rifle, and somehow the bullets never struck." He laughs. "His bullets always worked, though."

Their own best friends, the Smith boys kept their distance from other kids. "We felt we didn't really need anyone else," Vince says. "We had our gang right there." They were unusually shy children, but no one wondered where the family temperament came from: Vince's mother, Mavis, was painfully shy and withdrawn. Over the years, as her husband became more prominent and successful, she retreated further and further. "Sometimes it was just too much torture for Mavis to go out and meet people," says Hamilton.

"She was and is a very private person, highly self-contained," Vince says. "She is not the most expressive person. We knew the affection and love was there, but she was not demonstrative."

The entire family was dominated by the powerful presence of Otis Smith. Intelligent and shrewd, he had an enormous drive and boundless capacity for hard work. Yet whatever stature or success he attained, whatever celebrity he commanded, he never quite felt that he deserved it. Vince would come to terms with the legacy—at times overwhelming, and always inescapable—of being his father's eldest son.

Born in Memphis in 1922, Otis was raised along with his older brother, Hamilton, by their mother, Eva Grant Smith. A fiercely determined woman, she worked as a domestic for sixty years. After her own schooling ended in the sixth grade, she vowed to give her children the education they needed to escape her fate. She introduced her sons to the famous 1930s radio broadcasts of the Metropolitan Opera, delighting in Marian Anderson's "angelic voice." "A little teetotaling Methodist lady" is how Otis would later refer to his mother with affection.

Neither Otis nor his older brother knew their father, but from a very young age they recognized what would be the defining fact of their lives: He was white. To be a mixed-race child in the Deep South of the 1920s and 1930s was for Otis a source of great shame and confusion. Otis and Hamilton learned to parry the taunts of both whites and blacks, but they never shook a sense of displacement; they never felt they had claimed their rightful place in the world.

"My father had a courageous exterior," Vince says, "but there was an inner turmoil, which I think had a lot to do with growing up as a fair-skinned black at a certain time and place. You never quite belong." The psychological strain had a physical manifestation. By the age of twenty Otis had developed serious ulcers that he would battle the rest of his life.

While raising his own sons, Otis spoke rarely of his childhood, and never of his father. Vince and his brothers suspected the family secret, but Vince was thirty-three years old before Otis actually confirmed the fact by showing a photograph of his father. "These liaisons happen every now and again," Otis said, "and I wanted you guys to know." His tone was calm, as though he were discussing a vaguely troublesome cousin who was dropping by for Sunday dinner, but his sons knew the emotional truth behind that facade.

Occasionally, Otis would describe the physical hardships and poverty he confronted as a child. These stories made a strong impression on his sons, who had known only a comfortable, middle-class existence. His mother had moved the family seventeen times in fourteen years to keep ahead of bill collectors, Otis said, but even then, "Mother kept the house so clean you could eat off the floor." From the age of eight, both Otis and Hamilton worked odd jobs: selling peaches when they were boys, shoveling steel as young men.

Otis was offered a full-tuition scholarship from Morehouse College, but he had to turn it down because he had no money for room and board. Instead he made his way to Nashville, where he worked until he could afford to enroll in Fisk University, a local college. After three semesters, Otis enlisted in the army in October 1942. As one of the Tuskegee airmen, he served for a year under the command of General B.

O. Davis, who in 1936 had become the first black to graduate from West Point.

When his tour of duty ended, the G.I. Bill paid his way to Syracuse University. Otis was doing well and enjoying college life when one day he suddenly keeled over in class. A perforated ulcer was soon diagnosed. Otis took some time off, returned to Syracuse to complete his course requirements, and then moved on to Catholic University of America's law school in Washington, D.C., where he graduated in 1950.

A few years earlier, at a USO dance at Godman Field, Kentucky, Otis had met the woman who would become his wife. The couple married in 1949. Mavis was soon pregnant with their first child, which meant that Otis had to take a job on the assembly line at a GM plant. There were bills to pay; a suitable legal job would have to wait.

He didn't have to wait too long, though. Dudley Mallory, a 1926 graduate of the University of Michigan Law School, invited Otis to join his small practice on the north side of Flint. From 1950 to 1956, Mallory & Smith serviced the basic needs of local Buick plant employees who lived in this blue-collar neighborhood. Then, in 1957, Otis became an assistant prosecutor in Flint.

His public ambition soon flourished. During countless meetings at the local chamber of commerce, Otis deliberately and tirelessly honed his political connections. They eventually led him to Michigan's governor: G. Mennen Williams, an heir to the Mennen fortune who favored green polka-dot bow ties and answered to the nickname "Soapy." The governor was hardly an obvious mentor for Otis, but nevertheless he chose the role, naming Smith in 1957 to the chair of the Public Service Commission. "He recognized that a point in history had been reached where a black could claim that title, and he recognized that Dad was the man to do it," Vince says.

Two years later, Williams appointed Otis Smith state auditor general. Williams then became an undersecretary for African-American affairs in the Kennedy White House. His successor as governor, John Swainson, named Smith the first black justice of the Michigan Supreme Court. He was handily re-elected to that post in 1962 and 1964, but unexpectedly lost in 1966. "Court's Loss is General Motors'

Gain," pronounced the editorial page of the *Detroit Free Press*, and the family was especially proud to see the conservative *Jackson Citizen Patriot* declare that "Michigan's judicial system will sorely miss Otis Smith."

About seven months later came the call that would cap his career: Would Otis be interested in joining the legal staff of the General Motors Corporation? Not long after he took the job, Otis became the first black corporate officer at what was then the largest corporation in the U.S. Several years later, in 1977, he became the first black general counsel in the history of GM.

By the time his sons were born, Otis Smith was known and in many quarters revered throughout the state of Michigan. He took pride in his accomplishments, but he presented himself as a humble man. That was partly a matter of style; it would be unseemly, he felt, to boast or brag. But his humility also reflected an abiding fear that his work was never quite good enough. The fear kept him hungry, driving him to greater and greater success.

Otis Smith led his sons by example. That was his ideal of fatherhood, and he followed it with the same dogged devotion that he applied to any challenge. His actions spoke for him: Look at my life, see what hard work and determination have given me.

The words he used were often the sweet clichés and inspirational verses that his mother had repeated to him as a boy: "As the twig is bent, so is the tree inclined," among others. Invictus was a family anthem: "I am master of my fate, captain of my soul."

"You create your life, that was the lesson," Vince says. "You control your own destiny." Otis's values and expectations, and his exacting standards of excellence were absorbed at an early age. All the Smith sons would yearn for their father's approval.

He was not a harsh or punitive parent, and only rarely would he resort to corporal punishment. Otis Smith did not need such crude tactics to guide his sons along the proper path. "When he was angry, he had a terrifying look," Steve recalls. "He would bite his tongue, his eyebrows would get furrowed. He looked ferocious. You just didn't want to see that look again, so you did the right thing."

His work, though, was all-consuming. Most days Otis left the house at seven o'clock in the morning and returned about eight o'clock at night. Weekends were reserved for his sons, and their time together was intense. Friday nights were often spent at a local drive-in movie, with the boys stretched out in the back of the family station wagon, sharing Cracker Jacks and Cokes. In the long Michigan winters, weekends were filled with sledding, tobogganing, and ice skating in a local rink.

"He was without a doubt the critical influence on my life," says Vince, "but I thought it a simple relationship." He was always the dutiful son, incapable of even contemplating ordinary outbreaks of adolescent rebellion. Another teenager might have snuck off with his father's company car, but Vince enjoyed washing and polishing it on a quiet Saturday afternoon. "If I had an adolescent rebellion," Vince says with a smile, "I don't remember it." Though there was no clear, clean break between father and son, there was a period during Vince's first few years of college when he drifted away from his father's powerful orbit.

From Otis, Vince and his brothers had long felt a pressure to perform. It was a constant pressure, although not specific. "He didn't say go to this school, or take that degree," says Steven. For Vince and his brothers it was enough to know that they would follow in their father's footsteps.

In the end, though, none of the Smith boys came close to repeating their father's success. As Steve, the youngest, says, "Otis was a tough act to follow." Who could hope to journey even half the distance that Otis Smith had traveled in his life? Vince, who at forty-five bears an uncanny physical resemblance to his father at the same age, cannot speak so directly. The suggestion that Otis experienced even the mildest disappointment in his eldest son is unsettling to Vince, causing him to shift his long legs and sit up straight.

Holding himself apart from the family embrace beginning at an early age was Tony, the third son of Otis and Mavis Smith. His life story is a painful subject for his brothers.

"Being Otis Smith's son, people expect you to be able to walk on water," Tony once confessed to his uncle. After he left a prestigious Jesuit school in the ninth grade, he gradually began what would become an almost total retreat from society. One could see it as a repetition of his mother's isolation.

Tony lived in his parents' home until he was past the age of thirty. He never married, never graduated from college, never found any kind of a calling. Until recently he did not even own a telephone. "His inner circle became smaller and smaller," says his younger brother, Steve, "his world is so tightly wound. " "Maybe the early signs were misread by our parents and by me," Vince says. "Tony was a superb natural athlete, highly inquisitive, well-meaning. He just couldn't put the pieces of the puzzle together," Vince says with empathy. Vince understood better than anyone else the powerful expectations his father had set before all his sons.

"My father hoped that one of us would become a lawyer, though none of us did. I don't think he saw that as a source of disappointment." There is a slight pause. His body does not move, but his eyes look away. "Well, maybe he felt that at one point, but certainly not in his later years . . ."

"When it became apparent that I was not going to rise to my father's level," Vince says, "I knew that I had to somehow carry on the good name we were blessed with."

A love of music was a simpler gift that Otis passed on to his sons. From the time Vince first picked up a trumpet at the age of seven, music was an important part of his life. A few years later, he switched to piano and began picking out Motown tunes. When Vince was thirteen, the brothers formed a band, with Vince on electric piano, Raymond on bass, Tony on drums, and Steve on electric guitar. (Steve later became an accomplished amateur who played at the Montreux jazz festival).

Motown was in full force when the Smith family arrived in Detroit in 1967, and the family enjoyed its own little connection to the empire: Otis Smith played golf with Berry Gordy, the legendary founder of

Motown, and was a good friend of his sister, Esther. One afternoon, Vince and his brothers talked their way into making some demo records for Robert Gordy, Berry's brother. (Marvin Gaye happened to be sitting in the control room, and he heard them play.)

The University of Michigan, where Otis served as a regent from 1967 to 1971, was Vince's first choice for college. Though he traveled only forty miles from Detroit to the Ann Arbor campus, his first move away from home was liberating. By the end of his first semester, Vince had begun his first serious relationship with a woman.

He was a talented basketball player ("He had a hell of a hook," his brother Steven recalls), good enough to dream about a professional career. Then in 1971, during the summer after his junior year, a freak accident changed the course of Vince's life.

Vince had taken a job as a sign painter, just a little work to help the time pass in the sticky Michigan summer. Standing on a tall ladder, Vince was painting the words "Industrial Salvage" in dark blue lettering on a pale gray background about eighteen feet off the ground. The ladder was placed a few feet away from a garage, where a diesel truck was parked. Oblivious, the driver backed out and knocked the ladder down. As he realized that he was falling onto hard gravel, Vince let out a terrified scream.

He was about six foot five then, and he weighed about two hundred pounds. If Vince had landed on his head—later, in the hospital, he forced himself to visualize such a fall—the accident would almost certainly have killed him. As it was, his weight bore down on his right arm, shattering his elbow.

"As I felt the ladder falling backward, I said to myself, 'My goodness, I'm falling. It's twenty feet to the ground. I'll probably die.'" Vince blacked out as he fell, regaining consciousness for just a moment on the ground. "A man stood behind me and placed his hand on my back. 'Don't get up,' he said. 'The ambulance is coming, you're going to be okay.'" Vince heard a siren in the distance while experiencing an acute sensation of being totally disjointed in his right arm. Then he blacked out again.

Four operations over the course of the next seven months could not repair the damage. The elbow could never be properly reconstructed. Finally the surgeons gave Vince a stark choice: the arm could be set at a right angle to the ground or it could hang straight down, but either way, the position could never be changed. Vince chose the first option.

After a while, he learned to write with his left hand; strenuous rehabilitation lasted the better part of a year and a half. Before the accident, Vince had been a competitive swimmer working on perfecting his butterfly stroke. After the fall, in the pool for his physical therapy, he would feel the weight of his arm in the water. I'll never swim the butterfly now, he said to himself.

At first, he refused to even think about basketball. He would never know if he had the talent to make it as a pro, if he had been cheated of his real calling. So be it, Vince said to himself, suddenly middle-aged at twenty-one.

Otis took charge of the legal battles. They sued the owner of the building and the owner of the truck, and settlements were reached. Grateful for his father's support, Vince determined to confront his fate as Otis would have done. Visiting Vince in the hospital, his brothers saw a stoic figure. "I had bouts of 'why me,' but I never felt that too deeply. I knew I could become overwhelmed," Vince says. "He could have wallowed in self-pity, but he never did. He never complained," says Ray. Once again, Vince set a good example as the eldest son.

"In my more theatrical moments," Vince says wanly, "I say that I felt the cold hand of death on my shoulder. You know the scene in *Don Giovanni*, where Death approaches Don Juan? I learned that life, in its great beauty, can be taken from us at any time."

No one has ever described Vince as frivolous. A basic sobriety never leaves him. In the wake of the accident, though, he became more lighthearted. In his early twenties, Vince developed a persona that his father never managed—a man about town who enjoys what money can buy.

It was at a boisterous late-night party that Vince first met Mary Tate. When she first spotted Vince, he was helping himself to five pieces of chicken. Mary, who was helping to cater the party and had underestimated the size of the crowd, grew increasingly agitated. Would there be any food left? Who was this tall man who was making life so difficult?

Vince and Mary talked briefly that evening, but it was not until a year later, when they bumped into each other on the street, that they went out on their first date. Less than three months later, on Christmas Eve of 1976, they married. Vince and Mary were both twenty-five years old at the time.

Like many blacks of her generation, Mary was the daughter of parents raised in the deep South. In the late 1940s the couple had migrated to Detroit, where Mary's father worked as a construction laborer and served as an elder in a Pentecostal church. Mary was the middle child of five and the only girl, adored by all of her brothers.

She is vivacious, with bright brown eyes and an engaging smile. Capable and competent, she fights for what she wants and usually manages to inspire others to rally behind her. To that end she relies upon her energy, self-confidence, and more than a modest dose of her mother's Southern charm.

When they married, Vince had already begun his first full-time job at General Motors, his father's beloved company. Vince landed his job as a trainee on Pontiac's sales staff in the ordinary fashion, calling in to the central personnel office and filling out the necessary forms. His father knew nothing about it. This was but one moment in a long saga in which father and son silently kept their distance. Vince never asked for his father's professional help, and Otis never offered it.

"As someone who had to chase down whatever he had, my father believed that you've got to learn to be on your own," Vince says. "He recognized that my brothers and I—well, you could extend that and say young black males—we had to be able to stand on our own feet. I never wanted anyone to see me as other than myself."

It was not long before this noble principle was put to the test. In 1977, after Vince had spent three years working for GM in Detroit, the company moved him to California. In Oakland he and Mary lived in a small, cozy house while Vince worked as a customer relations supervisor for the Cadillac division. By the spring of 1981, though, GM was reeling as it belatedly came to grips with low-cost competition from Japan. A sweeping downsizing effort that year was just the beginning of a decade filled with layoffs.

Even though Vince did not hold a position covered by the UAW union when he was laid off in May 1981, he imagined that he would be recalled within a few months. Others shared that hope, but for Vince it never happened. He would have to find his livelihood outside the familiar fold of the General Motors Corporation.

Psychologically, that was no simple task. To accept the reality of his situation was a long and painful process. Vince had been doing well at GM, and he had what seemed to him to be reasonable expectations of a good future with the firm.

Most of all, General Motors was his father's company. It was home. Coworkers in the morning coffee line were always impressed to learn that Vince was the son of Otis Smith. How could Vince be angry at GM, which had bestowed upon his father the crowning moment of his career? "I said to myself, I have such a strong tie to this great company, in which I have an obviously good name," Vince recalls. "Someone will pull me out of the quicksand. But no one did."

During this period, both father and son stayed true to their wordless pact. Otis would not step forward to help his son, and Vince would never ask why. Even after he left GM, and his career floundered for several years, Vince never reached out to Otis for anything more than moral support.

When the shock of the GM layoff subsided, though, a deep depression set in. Weeks would go by, and Vince would be no closer to finding a new job. After about a year, Vince and Mary separated, and they came close to divorcing.

Six months after Vince lost his job, Mary was laid off by Ford as part of a general downsizing. She had been working as an administrative assistant in the Lincoln-Mercury division. Her boss had made her life miserable; it was no surprise when he added her name to the layoff list.

For a few weeks Mary seethed (she was just a few months short of a ten-year vesting period for pension benefits), and then she moved on. After about a month she landed a job at Honeywell, where she found a black woman mentor who inspired her own successful career as an executive.

Mary's salary at first was minimal, though, and she urged Vince to be more self-confident and aggressive about looking for work. "He could hold his own with princes and presidents, and yet he sold himself short," she says.

During this difficult period, Mary found it hard to fathom why Vince did not ask his father for financial help. "If my father had had the money, I would've picked up the phone in a minute. But Vince was trying to be a man and stand on his own." Mary didn't berate Vince about not calling Otis, though, and Vince never mentioned his father's name.

For more than a year, they lived apart. Helpless to pull her husband out of his depression, Mary hoped that the separation would force him to take some positive action. Maybe this will light a fire under him, she said to herself at the time. Instead, Vince grew more despondent.

As the months wore on, Vince learned that he could, in fact, survive on his own—and in an odd way, this helped him find a way back to his wife. At a critical juncture, neither Vince nor Mary could face the finality of divorce. They had barely known each other when they married; now, ten years later, they determined to start over. It was a gradual reconciliation, but it held. Their marriage was never threatened again.

Reunited with his family, Vince discovered in himself a new determination. When someone passed on a lead about a job at Chrysler, he quickly followed up and landed a position as a district sales manager in San Francisco. Vince worked with about twenty car dealers, selling them as many Chrysler products as he could. The popular models needed no endorsement, but "peddling the least desirable iron" was the challenge. Vince managed fairly well, but after a while he decided that he wanted to spend less time on the road—and, ideally, find a way out of sales.

He received offers from Dean Witter and AT&T. Dean Witter

offered more money, but the job was in sales and required a lot of cold calling. And so, in the spring of 1986, Vince took a pay cut to become a customer service representative for AT&T.

Vince's patience proved a valuable asset in his new job, as his bosses expected it would. His modest, polite demeanor was well suited to deflecting angry customer complaints, and Vince turned out to be a naturally gifted teacher as well. His avuncular manner and unflagging cheerfulness made him a skillful instructor of first-time customer representatives. After about a year, Vince was sent to help with a training program in San Antonio, where he received the highest score of all the traveling instructors (3.8 on a scale of 1 to 4).

In 1989 Vince was promoted to assistant staff manager and transferred to New Jersey. This was a mandatory appearance: virtually all AT&T managers are expected to spend some time working at the Basking Ridge headquarters or at one of the company's many New Jersey operations.

When the layoffs began a few years later, though, this move would seem disastrous. Vince had left his network of contacts and descended into the baffling bureaucracy that is the AT&T empire in northern New Jersey.

———————

The impending relocation sparked an immediate crisis. Over the course of a decade, Vince and his wife helped raise eight foster children in addition to their daughter, Yvonne, and their son, Stephen. In moving to New Jersey, they would leave behind Dion, a foster child with whom they had formed an especially close bond. Dion had lived with Vince's family between the ages of two and four.

Vince and Mary considered adoption, but concluded somewhat guiltily that they couldn't assume this obligation. Of course, Dion didn't understand why they all couldn't move together from California to New Jersey. "Don't go, don't go," he cried. "I'll be better."

Dion was adopted by a wonderful woman in her fifties who was able to unite the boy with his sister, whom she also adopted. Vince and Mary vowed to sustain their relationship with Dion, and to provide financial support as well. Inevitably, the separation still proved traumatic. After Dion had some counseling, Vince says, "he understood that there was a lot of love where he was and that he didn't lose the love of his Daddy Vince and Nana Mary." The boy sees Vince and Mary, who became his godparents, twice a year; he also knows that if anything ever happened to his adoptive mother, they would take him in. "We'd ensure his growth to manhood," Vince says as he glances at a recent photo of Dion, grinning in a baseball cap.

Arriving in Basking Ridge, Vince found himself one of tens of thousands of first-level managers. He worked in a staff organization whose function was to support the efforts of the company's field offices, providing them with information, services, and products to better serve their local customers. It was a classic middleman position: your ostensible function is to support the branches, but your more important job is to make your own office look good. This tension between the larger interests of the organization and the narrower interests of one's own fiefdom arises every day in corporate bureaucracies. Successful careers are built by balancing those competing claims.

That particular talent eluded Vince for most of his career. He was burdened, too, by a kind of naive decency. "You could say that he had too much integrity," says Sharon Miller, one of Vince's colleagues. "He had the desire to do it—whatever 'it' was, for all the right reasons. But that integrity could create problems." One episode she cites involved a reference manual in the office, which Vince and his colleagues were supposed to consult to answer various questions from the field. Having spent time in the outposts of the empire, she and Vince were eager to make headquarters more responsive. The reference manual had been written by managers in the office who had no experience in the field, and it showed. Vince tried to change it, investing time and energy well beyond the call of duty. But the code of the organization dictated that the old manual would prevail.

"I admired Vince," says his former colleague. "He never looked for glory. He just wanted to do a good job."

Still, he did have some political savvy—one could not spend years walking the corridors of GM, Chrysler, and AT&T without developing some instinct for corporate survival. And so it was that Vince picked up the downsizing rumors in the fall of 1992. His organization, Consumer Communications Services (CCS), which included the company's core long distance service, was careening toward layoffs.

"I called a few folks that I knew," Vince said, "and I told them, 'The ground is shifting here. Anything over there?' About four days later I interviewed with a hiring manager, who heard encouraging words about me from the people I knew on his staff. And that is how I found myself working in product management—specifically, in the internal billing systems for directory assistance." The job, in a different corner of the CCS division, carried the same title and the same salary as his old job. Would it bring more security? Vince could only hope.

But this new assignment ultimately proved to be anything but a safe haven. By the spring of 1993, Vince says, "we started to hear rumors. There may be this kind of staff cut, there may be that kind of reorganization. Batten down the hatches, that was the long and the short of it. I was no stranger to this, of course. There was my experience at GM, Mary's layoff at Ford. When the storm clouds started to gather, I thought, oh boy, here we go again."

Tucked away in his corner of the bureaucracy, Vince could still glimpse larger forces at work. During the last quarter of 1993, Joe Nacchio took control of CCS and moved quickly to undo the handiwork of his predecessor, who had been nudged aside. Nacchio—blunt, tough, a quick study—had left many organizations churning in his wake, and he was about to start the waters roiling at CCS. One of his first and most successful missions was the "True" series of calling plans, which reclaimed market share in the wake of MCI's successful "Friends and Family" advertising campaign.

With that success, however, came a restructuring. The head count at CCS would have to come down. Who would go?

Vince had been getting solid but not stellar performance reviews (the workplace equivalent of B's and C's) during his New Jersey years. "I was doing reasonably well and got along with everyone, but my reviews were not exceptional."

Surrounded as he was by dozens of fifteen-year company veterans, Vince imagined that his eight years of service marked him with a particular stigma. He was too familiar to qualify as the fresh-faced outsider that AT&T, like all insular organizations, so admired. Nor was he sufficiently seasoned to receive any of the considerable benefits of seniority. "I knew that if the choice was between an eight-year person . . . and a fifteen-year person whose fast track days were gone, the other fellow would win," Vince says. "I had to assume I'd be on the list."

Unbeknownst to Vince, his modest chances of surviving the layoff had been further weakened by the system's cool impersonality. When executives met to sort out the survivors and the victims, Vince's most important boss, district manager Stephanie Brienza—two steps above him in the hierarchy, and the person who best knew his value to the organization—was kept out of the conversation. This was not official policy: sometimes managers were allowed to make pleas for their people, and sometimes they weren't. For Vince, though, it meant that his professional fate was sealed by men and women who did not know him at all.

"It was a secret group," says one second-level manager who knows both Vince and his district manager. "There were division-level managers and directors [the fourth and fifth levels in the AT&T hierarchy]. They simply decided, 'These are the functions we need going forward.'"

In the end, it appeared to some insiders that the group hit hardest by the layoff were first-level managers such as Vince. Defenders of the downsizing argued that this change was appropriate and overdue; and indeed AT&T had tacked on far too many low-level managers and supervisors over the years. But the decision also reflected the crude bias of many bureaucracies: left to their own devices, the bosses often take care of their own.

During the 1996 downsizing, the company formalized this process of identifying layoff victims. In the critical conversations (known as roundtable discussions), employees would be represented by their boss's boss—that is, managers two steps ahead on the organizational ladder.

Still, many employees were either saved or sabotaged by virtual strangers.

Stephanie Brienza delivered the bad news with grace. She was sorry, she said, she regretted the fact that Vince was, in the jargon, "at risk."

Given a sixty-day grace period to find another job within the company, Vince put himself through the requisite paces. He called on the flimsiest of connections for job prospects, combed through the data banks at the AT&T outplacement center, and dutifully noted prospects inside and outside AT&T. As he had predicted, he was burdened by the fact that he was relatively new to AT&T's New Jersey job network; in California, there would have been more people to extend a hand.

Vince was particularly grateful for several job leads passed along by a coworker who was in even more dire straits. Chris, a sixteen-year AT&T veteran, had been declared "at risk" only a few hours after his wife, another AT&T staffer, heard the same news. In the final months of a difficult pregnancy, she became so distraught that she had to be rushed to a hospital. As it happened, the couple found other jobs in the organization, but Vince did not.

"Vince conducted himself as he always had," Chris recalls. "He was professional and calm. You never saw him lose his temper. Plenty of people were ranting and raving, but Vince never did."

His last day at AT&T arrived. "When it happens," Vince says, "you ponder the fact that you've prepared for this, after a fashion. And now the day is here." At nine-thirty on the morning of March 31st, he met with Stephanie, making strained conversation for about forty-five minutes. "I've been down this road before," Vince told her, "and I have every intention of pulling through."

He was driving home south on Interstate 287, his usual route, when the thought seized him: We must keep this news from Dad. Otis Smith was in the final stages of terminal cancer then. Vince decided to keep word of the layoff from both his parents and two of his three brothers, confiding only in Raymond.

This rejection did not seem as personal to Vince as the layoff from

GM; AT&T was not his father's company. Inevitably, though, he was shaken. For Vince the crisis would be defined and resolved by one central fact: he was the eldest son of Otis Smith.

"Was the layoff fair? Was the downsizing just? I asked myself those questions, but I dared not dwell upon them. Is anything fair in life? I knew I had to land on my feet," Vince says. "That was my job. As a husband and father, as the oldest sibling, I felt this was a duty I owed to a select group of nice people. I made a deliberate decision to separate my extrinsic value from my intrinsic self-worth."

Those were his conscious, rational thoughts. The more powerful feeling was unconscious. When his elbow had shattered, when he had faced his first downsizing at General Motors, at any moment when his life was in turmoil, the words would float through his mind like shadows on the water: *You are your father's son. Be strong.*

Vince had been out of work for a while when an old AT&T friend, a district manager in another division, revealed to Vince that he had been earning considerably less than employees with similar performance records and equivalent seniority. "I had to leave the company to find out how little I was being paid," Vince says. "It was a bit of a shock. I had no idea they were getting me as cheaply as they were."

Was race a factor? Vince chooses not to think so, but he admits that his wife, Mary, "is much quicker to call the race card." She was livid, in fact. "They treated you unfairly," she told Vince. An AT&T spokesman will say only that company policy explicitly prohibits any form of racial discrimination.

Vince spent much of the next three months in Detroit with his father. "Had I not been in this predicament, I would not have been able to spend these days with Dad that I so very much wanted. I felt that I had to find something of substance to hang onto." Unconsciously reaching for a metaphor that recalls his own accident, he adds, "It's like you're hanging over a precipice, and you've got one arm free, but you can't use the other. So you'd better latch on to something."

Otis Smith's final months were spent in considerable pain. "There were moments," his son Ray recalls, "when he'd break down and confess his fear. We'd have a good cry. That was quite uncharacteristic; he had never before shown any fear in the face of adversity." At the same time, Otis prepared his sons for his death. "I had no unanswered questions," says Vince. "That's one reason I could cope with his passing as well as I did. And I say quite proudly that when my time comes, when I cross the river, the first person I will see is my father, and I will shake his hand."

Five days after the funeral, Vince returned home. One siege had ended, while another had just begun. It would be more than a year before Vince would find a new job.

Grief finds its own rhythm. For Vince, the mourning was slow and steady, a constant presence. For a while, Vince thought of nothing but his father's life and death. There was no immediate financial pressure: Otis left his sons a modest inheritance, and Mary found herself promoted several times in the year and a half that Vince was unemployed.

Vince looked for a position in customer service, where most of his career had been spent. The skill is transferable across different industries—managing angry customers in the auto industry, for instance, is not very different from handling irate health care clients. Vince's calm, unflappable demeanor, readily apparent to any prospective employer, was an obvious asset.

But despite dozens of interviews and a few tentative nibbles, there were no solid offers of work. Vince kept himself busy, rising at five-thirty reading the business press. As the months wore on, Mary remembered well the strain that Vince's first layoff had caused, and she controlled any impulse to urge her husband to move faster.

Vince appeared to family and friends alike to be coping remarkably well. Still, the reality of the corporate world could be sobering. At the Time Warner headquarters, Vince filled out an application in the personnel department. "'Let me take this upstairs right away,' this nice lady told me. I thought I was getting some kind of special treatment," Vince recalls. "And of course she was just doing her job. Then she said, 'You'll hear from someone within three weeks.' And of course three weeks turned into three months, and then it was a short, 'No, thank you.'"

After about twelve months of unemployment, Vince felt the first stirrings of real panic. The early evening could be exquisitely difficult. "My son would come home from school. I'd watch some TV news and hear the events of the day, and all of a sudden it hits you—another day in the life of the world has gone by, and you were on the bench."

"In my darker moments, I'd wonder, 'Is there a place for me? Is there ever going to be a place for me?' You start asking yourself all the what-ifs."

Vince compared the self-doubt to a creeping spider: "You'd feel it moving up your back. For the first couple of seconds, it's tickling your back, and you say, 'Oh, there's something back there,' but you don't know what it is. Then it hits a certain point along your spine and suddenly it's obvious—you've got a spider crawling up your back, and if you don't get something quick, pretty soon you're going to have a web around you."

Around this time, the spider started creeping up Mary's back, too. "My wife was a great support to me," Vince says, "but around the one-year mark it seemed to Mary as though I had lost my zeal. It occurred to her, maybe nothing is going to happen."

Though Vince had impressed several of Mary's colleagues and superiors, he had balked at the thought of going to work for his wife's company, a health care insurer. A rising star at the firm, Mary also wanted to be careful that she was not using her influence to get her husband a job. She made an initial introduction, but then she stepped back. Vince went through the interview and application process, and finally—sixteen months after he left AT&T—he signed on as a senior account manager.

In his new position, Vince became part of a team that services the problems of large accounts. A benefits manager at ABC Technology Corporation, for example, calls to complain about the fact that someone on her staff has been refused reimbursement for what appears to be a standard procedure. Vince's job is to listen, seem sympathetic, and determine the legitimacy of the request. Then he must manipulate his own company's systems to solve the client's problem as quickly as possible. He is a middleman, patiently scuttling between bureaucracies.

The health care firm is young, growing rapidly, and very profitable. Most employees are in their late twenties and early thirties. "I sometimes think of myself as a young Turk and then I remind myself, 'Hey, wait a minute, they're twenty-eight and you're forty-five.' But it has rejuvenated me."

Still, he often plays the role of patient father figure. To some degree "I'm looked on as a steadying [influence]. I don't have the industry knowledge that these kids have, having grown up in the business. But they'll look in amazement at me when some client flies off the handle and I don't get all frazzled or riled up. It's partly demeanor and partly good old-fashioned seasoning."

Though his under-thirty colleagues are hardworking and "genuinely thrilled to be with this organization," Vince says, "they are smart enough to say to themselves, 'Hmm, things could change.' They know they won't be there forever."

Vince is not so nonchalant; he aspires to a detachment he hasn't quite mastered. He still feels a faint echo of the powerful devotion he felt for GM and AT&T. "Loyalty is still a meaningful word for me," Vince says. "I refuse to abandon, as I wish not to be abandoned."

Clearly Vince was hardened by the AT&T downsizing, though he has never been a cynical person. "I was so careful in my own little domain at AT&T," Vince says. "The mistakes I made didn't go much further than my desk. So I do find it ironic that the people who made mistakes of the billion-dollar variety float away on golden parachutes."

For himself, Vince imagines a different kind of motion. "I suppose we should see our careers as riding the waves. I'd like to think [that] with a decent record, I'll be safe. But, hey, it's happened twice before; I had a decent record and I wasn't safe. So ride the wave for as long as you can, because one day you could be washed up on shore."

As Vince molds his new identity as a different sort of company man, he has very modest expectations. "At this point," he says, "I don't expect to find personal validation in my work. Have I always been a fish out of water in the corporate world? Perhaps. I will do my job responsibly, but I will not look to any organization to reassure me of my self-worth, to tell me who I am."

Survivors of three major downsizings between them, Vince and Mary appreciate that, like so many others, they have been buffeted by forces beyond anyone's control. By the mid-1990s, though, the winds were blowing in their direction.

When Mary joined the fast-growing company where she and Vince now work, she received stock options whose value soared with the growth of HMOs and the bull market. After several years, she cashed them in; combined with some of the inheritance that Otis had left his sons, the couple had the money to build a splendid, Southern-style house in central New Jersey. Light and airy, it has a winding wooden staircase and a magnificent twenty-foot cathedral ceiling in the living room. For Vince and Mary, the house stands as a symbol of their life together, and of the commitment that carried them through a difficult year.

To redefine his identity in the wake of the downsizing was for Vince a long struggle. He found his strength in the simplest truths of his life: he is a husband, a father, and—finally and always—the eldest son of Otis Smith.

3   AT&T: A CHANGING
CORPORATE CULTURE

If we don't tell the truth about ourselves, someone else will.

—Theodore Vail, creator of the Bell System and AT&T president, 1907–1919

Though they never met one another, the six protagonists of this book shared a certain kinship as employees of AT&T. AT&T attracted and cultivated a particular breed of company man and woman, for whom loyalty and a sense of collective purpose were genuine and deep. These six men and women came to appreciate the unique history and corporate culture which engendered those feelings. They came to understand, too, in the most intimate way, how and why that culture is coming undone.

After thirty-six years, Jim Meadows was retiring from AT&T—"taking the package," in the corporate lexicon. At the age of fifty-eight, he was also traversing the path from the old working world to a new one.

Jim was the archetype of the unquestioning, uncomplaining company man, moving his wife and children for AT&T eleven times through Oregon, Seattle, North Carolina, Boston, St. Louis, Los Angeles, and San Francisco. "I never influenced the moves," he says, "and I never resisted the moves." A trim, gray-haired man in a gray suit, Jim looks the part he has played for so many years—the affable, hardworking executive who gets the job done.

At his farewell party at the Old Mill Inn in Basking Ridge, New Jersey, in the spring of 1996 colleagues teased Jim about his predictable work schedule: in at six-thirty, impatient for the first morning meeting. There was the obligatory slide show, with photos of the houses Jim had bought over the years, each one a bit grander than the one that came before. In the background someone played Frank Sinatra singing "My Way."

Jim Meadows is convinced that his career is an artifact. The thirty-five-year company man will soon be extinct.

As a human resources vice president at AT&T, Jim became a proselytizer for what he believes to be the organization of the future. It will have few jobs in the usual sense—certainly nothing like a career. People will hopscotch among projects and teams, both within a company and among companies. "The whole concept of the defined job is basically obsolete," he says. "It is being replaced by fields of work."

Jim Meadows nudged AT&T toward this imagined future back in 1991, when he introduced a program called Resource Link. AT&T "associates" who belong to Resource Link keep the standard employee benefits, but they are not part of any business unit; instead, they migrate from one temporary assignment to another. Creating this program is Jim's greatest pride, although it is not what earned him his greatest renown. In the middle of AT&T's 1996 downsizing, Jim became best known as "the man who wrote the package"—the policies that governed employees' severance benefits, the same "package" that he would soon take himself.

Many AT&T veterans in their fifties who leave the company (willingly or not) suffer a penalty in their pension; unless a manager is fifty-five or older, the company slashes a sliding discount off his retirement benefits. Jim, though, was lucky. When he walked away, he took with him a full pension as well as medical insurance, which will last for the rest of his life.

He also stepped into a nice second career with Lee Hecht Harrison, the outplacement agency that has handled AT&T downsizings for years. From his new base in Tampa, Jim helps his new employer sell programs like Resource Link to other corporations. "Internal variable workforces, that's what we're working to establish," he says.

Jim's retirement party in 1996 felt like the old days, though it was not so long ago that AT&T would have paid for the farewells. Leaving the club, some of the guests got caught in a sudden spring downpour. As they drove along the leafy roads, a rainbow appeared. It seemed a fitting coda to the warmth of the evening.

The next day, though, behind the closed doors of AT&T's human resources department, Jim's former coworkers could be heard grumbling about his new situation. The man gave preliminary approval to Lee Hecht Harrison's outplacement contract with AT&T, and now he was leaving to *work* for Lee Hecht Harrison?

Jim pointed out to anyone who asked that he did not look for this job—Harrison's parent company approached him several months after he had already decided to retire from AT&T. Nor was Jim ever involved in negotiating the specific terms of the agency's contract with AT&T.

People liked Jim and they wished him well, and certainly he had done nothing that violated any company policy. Still, there was something unsettling about the arrangement. Eventually, though, his colleagues came to the relatively benign conclusion that Jim was simply cashing in his chips, making use of his reputation, and "managing his career."

On a raw afternoon in late March, about eight weeks before Jim Meadows's retirement party, the casualties of AT&T's 1996 downsizing were attending a company-sponsored job fair at New Jersey's Raritan Valley Community College. Like Jim Meadows, the men and women who paced the floor of a converted basketball court also spoke about managing their careers, but their voices betrayed more anxiety than conviction.

Trying to reclaim some of its reputation as a benevolent employer, AT&T had dispatched staffers at Lee Hecht Harrison to help organize the event. They attracted a respectable turnout: fifty-eight hiring companies and nearly three hundred would-be employees.

No one smiled.

At the center of the scene stood Janice Cooley, an unflappable middle manager in AT&T's Human Resources department. For five years, she had been running the company's main outplacement center (more hopefully described as a "resource" center).

A visitor gestured toward the crowd. "They say they love the company, they still love AT&T."

"Yes." Janice replied, too exhausted to hide the strain of the day. "They do. It breaks their hearts even more."

Jim Meadows was lucky enough to find a better exit. As they move away from the old working world, where loyalty and community still had some meaning, Jim and his brethren know that they must look to their own self-interest. But it is a sensitive transition they face.

AT&T is itself at a pivotal point of transition, both in the substance of its business and in the spirit of its corporate culture. The company must take advantage of and at the same time transcend its past as a regulated monopoly providing universal telephone service. It must now stake its claim in a deregulated, fast-changing telecommunications industry recently beset by a series of mergers and takeovers that have transformed the landscape. After years of floundering, AT&T must shore up its position in its core long distance and wireless business, conceive and execute a strategy for entering the local U.S. phone markets, move aggressively overseas, and bolster its flanks on the Internet.

AT&T had endured more than a decade's worth of glaring missteps and plain bad luck. These are embodied most starkly in restructuring charges—more than $19 billion worth—taken during the tenure of chairman Bob Allen (1988–1996). In late 1997 AT&T's board of directors announced that Michael Armstrong, the chief executive of Hughes Electronic, would replace Allen as AT&T's chairman and CEO. Within weeks of the announcement, Allen's career had ended and his legacy looked more dubious than ever.

When Armstrong took charge—remarkably, he was the first outsider to lead Ma Bell—AT&T seemed in a state of chaos. A brand name that once had extraordinary power and resonance had been sadly debased. AT&T was fighting for its future.

The old corporate culture, which valued stability, security, and a sense of shared purpose, has been slowly disappearing since the breakup of the Bell System in 1984. In its place is a diffuse but palpable confusion, as the organization and its employees sort out whatever mutual claims and obligations might yet survive. Workers believe they must protect and pursue their own individual interests. "I must manage my career," so many of them repeat to themselves, never entirely sure what the words mean. The process is neither simple nor egalitarian—especially at a company like AT&T, where power remains very much concentrated at the top of the organizational chart.

Nevertheless, many AT&T employees still feel a personal attachment to the firm. "For some reason," says Jim Meadows, "after all AT&T has been through, the company inspires tremendous loyalty. It defies everything you think would happen."

For many people, that loyalty is rooted in an honest affection for the company's past. AT&T operated what was, without question, the finest phone system in the world. The scale and the scope of the enterprise in 1983 was vast: 1 million employees, 3 million shareholders, and $138 billion in assets, making AT&T the wealthiest private institution in the world.

And it was an exceptional company. AT&T was a regulated utility, after all, not a mere profit-making enterprise. And it sold not cardboard boxes or soap powder, but telephones, which allow people to talk to each other. It gave generously to deserving causes, and its employees were good citizens, pitching in with every small-town charity drive.

Employees who joined AT&T before the 1982 consent decree to break up the Bell System (in 1996, they still represented the majority of the workforce) believed that they had dedicated themselves to a worthy cause, a cause that had little to do with money. "People of my generation have a fond memory for the particular spirit that was here," says Burke Stinson, a fifty-six-year-old AT&T spokesman who joined the company in 1969. "You weren't a crass commercial person, you were working for a higher order, for something that was terribly important. The company encouraged that [attitude]."

Employees look back with respect at the power of the company's mission. It was not public-relations posturing or mere words on a company handout; it was a real idea that people believed in. It began with the simplest notion: everyone should have a telephone. Eventually, as telephone service became virtually ubiquitous, the basic mission became to sell the highest-quality products and offer the finest customer service.

This coherent corporate vision was reflected in the organization of the huge company. Individual divisions and departments were essentially atoms of a single molecule; policies and procedures, standards and technology were uniform and inviolate. The company's philosophy was distilled in the words of Theodore Vail, the visionary who created the Bell System: "One system. One policy. Universal service."

An AT&T executive in his mid-forties whose father also was a company veteran offers this observation: "People can't let go of the old spirit. They say to themselves, 'In my little sphere of influence, in my little department, the company still represents service and honesty and integrity.' People hold onto that idea, because they see it as something that was good. It's not necessarily there anymore, but they can't let go."

That devotion reflects both denial and self-preservation. The impulse is to ignore the plain reality that a sense of shared purpose has been irrevocably lost. At the same time, people still need that basic connection, a sense of citizenship in a larger community.

While blue-collar telephone operators and factory workers (occupational employees, the company calls them) had suffered cyclical layoffs for decades, AT&T managers—those employees not covered by a union contract—came as close to lifetime job security as one could get in corporate America. Their counterparts at IBM and Eastman Kodak shared that security, and a handful of other large firms offered close approximations.

One could see the virtue in stability and still recognize that at AT&T it eventually produced a sluggish, insular bureaucracy. Over the years, the organization instinctively rewarded caution and deference and viewed the unexpected with suspicion. Why have two committees when you could have four? Decisions that might take days at a smaller, less hidebound firm would drag on for months at AT&T.

The almost limitless resources of the old monopoly encouraged a breathtaking grandiosity. Ed Block, who joined Southwestern Bell in 1952 and retired from AT&T as a senior vice president in 1986, witnessed the evolution of this corporate spirit. "Over time," he says, "success insinuated into the culture a sense that God made the Bell System. Any change could only disrupt God's order."

Over the years, promising new products were created and then abandoned, whether by default or design one could never be sure. "AT&T has had leading-edge technology, but it has struggled to get it to market," says David Barnes, a manager at AT&T Solutions, a consulting division within AT&T that advises outside companies on their telecommunications and technology networks.

Though scientists at Bell Labs invented the technology for the cellular telephone back in 1947, in the early 1980s AT&T woefully underestimated the potential demand for such phones. The 1984 breakup of the Bell System allowed AT&T to acquire a wireless phone company, but management did not make its move until long after the market had taken off. In 1994, to get back in the game, AT&T paid a steep price—$11 billion, plus $4.5 billion in assumed debt—to acquire McCaw Cellular.

From the moment that AT&T agreed to break up the Bell System, senior management preached the virtues of risk-taking. Top management demanded "out-of-the-box thinking" until employees laughed when they heard the overworked phrase. Scores of outsiders were hired, and teams of experts endlessly consulted. By this time, though, "any tendency toward entrepreneurship was pretty well smothered," Ed Block recalls. The institution had become tied up in its own rigidity, and imagination was almost guaranteed to be ignored.

The late 1980s and early 1990s brought repeated restructuring and reorganization at AT&T, along with waves of layoffs and management shuffles. The churning culminated in the company's "trivestiture," announced in September 1995, in which AT&T split into three pieces. Its troubled computer business reclaimed the old name of NCR, the firm AT&T had acquired back in 1991; the equipment group became Lucent Technologies, which has since flourished. The remaining divisions emerged as the "new" AT&T, though the majority of its revenues still derived from its century-old business of selling long-distance telephone service to residential and business customers.

Wall Street cheered the breakup, driving the stock up more than 10 percent on the day the news broke. Bob Allen was initially lauded for being bold and decisive in trying to "unlock" the value of the firm's assets. AT&T employees saw past the posturing: the breakup was a clear admission that the fundamental business strategy that had defined and directed the company for the past decade—a convergence of computers and telecommunications—had utterly failed.

"When the trivestiture was announced, we all knew it was the right thing to do. In fact, it was long overdue," says one AT&T manager. "But this was also the biggest admission that we [had] screwed it all up!"

Amid this turbulence came the company's largest downsizing, the proposed 40,000 job cuts that AT&T proclaimed on January 2, 1996. The company would cut about 70 percent of the jobs in 1996, and the rest in the following two years.

By the end of 1996, a year after the breakup, AT&T managed to appear both callous and bumbling. Of 17,000 jobs that were targeted for cuts at the new AT&T, only 5,700 had been shed. Lucent cut about 17,000 of its projected 23,000, although about 6,500 "disappeared" through outsourcing or the sale of business units. What's more, both the new AT&T and Lucent embarked on a rash of hiring, which meant that the total number of employees on the AT&T payroll remained roughly the same. (At Lucent, the payroll fell slightly, from 131,000 to 121,000.)

Then, in the spring of 1997, as its profits and stock price were tumbling, AT&T quietly announced that it would try again: a voluntary buyout offer would be followed by an involuntary downsizing if a quota was not met. Many employees saw AT&T management lurching between cynicism and lack of leadership. What had happened to this company, which had once been so mighty and important?

A HISTORY OF MAKING HISTORY

AT&T's story begins with one of the great bursts of American ingenuity: Alexander Graham Bell's invention of the telephone in 1876. History is often the product of chance connections, and they are certainly evident in the human drama that surrounds Bell's creation.

When the inventor was twelve years old, his mother began to go deaf. That trauma, it has been widely observed, instilled in Bell an empathy for the deaf which would be a defining fact of his life. Bell's father was a famous teacher of the deaf and Alexander followed his example for several years before he began his own scientific research. One of his students was Mabel Hubbard, a deaf woman who Alexander Graham Bell married when he was thirty years old.

It was March 10, 1876, after years of experiments, when Bell picked up the contraption that would be transformed into the telephone, and probably said (historians debate his exact words), "Mr. Watson, come here, I want to see you." In the first stroke of the good fortune that would color much of AT&T's early history, Bell filed the patents for his invention on the morning of February 14, 1876. That afternoon, a rival researcher, Elisha Gray, registered patents for his similar invention. Bell won the complicated and lengthy litigation that followed, well served by the fact that his father-in-law, Gardiner G. Hubbard, was a leading patent attorney. (Deeply embittered by his failure, Elisha Gray continued to work as an inventor, eventually amassing about seventy patents that actually paid him more money than Bell and his wife received from the telephone.)

Hubbard soon offered to sell the Bell patents to Western Union, then the largest company in the United States, for $100,000. Size and success had bred a classic corporate conceit in Western Union, and the suggestion was met with derisive laughter. But once it became clear that the telephone was more than a passing distraction, Western Union began to compete in the market. More litigation ensued between Bell and Western Union until a deal was drawn: Western Union would stay out of the telephone business, and Bell would steer clear of telegraphs.

Onto this stage walked Theodore Vail, the brilliant businessman who conceived and created the Bell System. Hubbard persuaded Vail to work for the owners of the Bell patents, which Vail did until he quit in 1887. Rehired when the business came under the control of the Morgan bank, Vail later served as AT&T president from 1907 to 1919. From the beginning, he understood that the power and value of the telephone lay not in the patents themselves but in the "interconnectedness" that enabled one phone to talk to another. He deliberately and rather audaciously set out to build a national communications network.

Vail was convinced that this network must be a monopoly. Expecting a swarm of rivals when the Bell patents expired in 1893 and 1894, he orchestrated the ingenious system in which Bell granted licenses to build and run local phone exchanges in return for an equity stake in the new local companies. "What we wanted to do," Vail later remarked, "was to get possession of the field in such a way that, patent or no patent, we could control it."

As Vail predicted, hundreds of start-ups began to sell phone service once the Bell patents expired. They tried to pick pieces off the Bell hide, rather like the small "dial-around" companies of the mid-1990s took market share from AT&T by buying bulk time on long-distance networks at discounted rates and reselling it to consumers.

By 1902, 1,500 firms controlled more than a million phones. Still, only the Bell System sold long-distance service, and it simply refused to connect a local exchange to its own network until the local phone company—having nowhere else to turn—acquiesced to AT&T's terms. This was raw monopoly power, powerfully enforced.

The core of the enterprise was established at the outset: vertical integration, as embodied in the union between technology and equipment, and the sprawling phone network. To this day AT&T employees refer to "the network" with quiet respect. Originally built on copper wires, the network eventually included microwave relay stations, fiber optics, and wireless exchanges. If the network formed the body of the company, though, its soul was the mission of universal service—low-cost, high-quality telephone service for every American household.

CREATING A CORPORATE CULTURE

AT&T could devote itself to customer service in part because its profits were guaranteed. In theory, government regulation, which dates back to the historic Kingsbury Commitment of 1913, ensured that AT&T would realize sufficient earnings to provide good service and give its stockholders a reasonable return. A debate predictably revolved around the definitions of "reasonable" and "good." The government's concept of fair pricing was based on the company's costs, which were passed along to the consumer.

A corporate culture sustains itself through the stories people tell. New AT&T employees would hear the worn-out tales of devoted service, the grand gestures well beyond the call of duty. Most famously, there was Angus MacDonald, the linesman who walked out onto the streets of Boston in the middle of a blizzard in 1888 to work on the phone lines. A painting of that scene was reproduced by the thousands and hung on office walls throughout the Bell System.

"It was a sort of corporate religion," says Glyn Bolar, who joined AT&T in 1974 and retired twenty-two years later as a business strategist. "You had to say the words, and mean them, in order to be accepted. They weren't printed on a mission statement. It was the credo of any good craftsman. If something is worth doing, it is worth doing well." That philosophy was possible as long as AT&T remained a regulated monopoly where costs were not an important concern.

Customer service, though, did not necessarily mean giving the customer what he or she wanted. "Often, AT&T would give the customer what AT&T, in its infinite wisdom, felt that he needed, whether it was a different phone or a new service," Bolar recalls. "Though it has to be said that the company's judgment was often correct." One in-house refrain was "We make it, you take it."

It was an inward-looking organization. What the customer wanted or needed had to be subservient to the scientific standards that defined the Bell System. Nothing could impinge, nothing could interfere to compromise those standards. When AT&T was ready to introduce the Princess telephone, it did; whether the average American might have liked it a year or two sooner was an irrelevance.

This was *noblesse oblige* more than dictatorial fiat. The essential paternalism of the institution extended to both customers and employees: Join our family, and we will take care of you.

The paternalistic family traditionally functioned as a class system, and in many respects it still does. People know their place in the hierarchy. "'Why should I talk to you?' 'What level are you?' You actually still hear those questions," says manager David Barnes.

About 45 percent of all staffers are occupational workers. They include operators, factory workers, and customer service representatives—all workers who are paid by the hour and covered by union contracts. More than half of all employees are classified as managers, though the immediate supervisors of occupational staff (the so-called A band, where 37 percent of the staff are ranked) may have little autonomy or responsibility.

The next rung (the B level, representing 15 percent of the payroll) includes such positions as assistant branch managers and computer programmers. A significant jump in status comes with the level of district manager (the C band), where about 4 percent of employees are ranked and many careers plateau. A branch manager in the field, or a marketing manager or product manager at headquarters, would fall in this group. About 1 percent of the staff make it to the level of division manager (the D band), whose ranks include lawyers, advertising executives, marketing and sales managers.

At the E level are AT&T's directors, who receive generous stock options, free financial advice, and assorted perks (including the universal symbol of corporate prowess, the personal parking space). A director might work as the leader of a strategy group, as a senior member of the public-relations department, or as the head of several regional offices.

Some of these directors are also called vice presidents, but, in the end-less folly of bureaucracies, at AT&T there are "real" vice presidents and pseudo vice presidents. Real vice presidents are officers of the company, and their status is signaled by the placement of a comma. "Vice president, Human Resources," belongs to a real vice president; "Human Resources, vice president" is the lesser label.

Like all large organizations, AT&T spawned distinct corporate cul-tures in its fiefdoms. There were separate clubs in the Bell System: Western Electric, with its research arm, Bell Labs; the long-distance di-vision, Long Lines; the operating companies (the future baby Bells); and an elite, smaller headquarters group, the General Departments, whose senior executives established the overall strategy for the firm.

Western Electric, the manufacturing division that had been acquired in 1882, was defined by the ethos of the engineer: Do it by the book, and do it right. Certainly Western Electric attracted the best engineers in the Midwest, earnest and hardworking young men from schools such as Carnegie Mellon and Iowa State. They found their life's work mastering the lines, switches, and wires that formed the telephone network.

With forty-four separate levels of management as late as 1983, Western Electric was absurdly hierarchical. It was also a notoriously in-flexible organization; rules and procedures were clearly stated and uni-formly obeyed.

The system produced first-class equipment. There was a strong in-centive for that, too: telephones were leased to customers, and repairs were free. The humble rotary telephone was an exceptional speci-men—twice as heavy as it needed to be, full of gold where a lesser metal would suffice. Yet AT&T could estimate its life at forty years (in its ac-counting, the company actually depreciated its investment over that period). Finally, Western Electric's factories served as the company's economic shock absorber. When demand was slack, workers were laid off and production lines were shut down.

Officially part of the manufacturing division—but set apart from the corporate infrastructure for most of its tenure—was the extraordi-nary research organization, Bell Labs. From the company's beginning, a research lab was part of the Bell System, which meant that the well-spring of innovation and technology was always an integral part of the enterprise.

In its prime, Bell Labs was an island of unfettered thinking and generously funded scientific research. Although the labs were also famous for the kind of petty politics that one finds at many academic institutions, the caliber of the staff was remarkable, and the roster of Bell Labs inventions (microwave relays and electronic switching, as well as the transistor) was unsurpassed by any other corporate research organization in the world.

Researchers at Bell Labs displayed open contempt for "the suits," as they referred to the managers at headquarters who controlled their budgets. The suits, for their part, saw the researchers as reckless spendthrifts. In 1992, a reorganization of the labs linked most of its research groups to business units at various outposts of AT&T. Although there had always been a subtle pressure on Bell Labs to develop products with commercial potential, now the directive was plain: inventions that had near-term commercial prospects claimed the highest priority. Pure research would continue, but it had become a luxury.

Still, the most radical and valuable inventions often require a long-term commitment of both time and capital; it may be impossible to predict what the demand for a product might be. But in the wake of the 1996 trivestiture, when Bell Labs became part of Lucent Technologies, pure research receded even farther as a corporate priority.

AT&T's Long Lines division, which operated the long-distance network, displayed the confidence that came with operating the world's finest phone system. "They were a proud, tight little band," Ed Block recalls. Within the Bell System, they achieved real autonomy. Block remembers sitting in on years of debates among the senior executives about how the local and long-distance networks should manage the transition from analog to digital technology in the mid-1970s. Long Lines, however, didn't wait for marching orders. "When Long Lines converted to digital, beginning in 1976," Block recalls, "they just did it. One day we looked around and, presto, we had an all digital network coast to coast. The analog switches had been junked."

The managers who ran the operating companies, the future baby Bells, aspired to similar independence, but they never quite achieved it. They were the men on the line, answering customer complaints, battling with local politicians, and reporting at the end of the day to the men at the top of the organizational pyramid. Between the managers of the General Departments and the local phone companies there was the static common to so many bureaucracies—the rift between officers up in headquarters and men and women down in the field. A central point of contention concerned the annual 2 percent levies imposed by AT&T on the operating companies. That debate reflected a deeper tension: the "real" phone company men saw the General Departments staff as pampered bureaucrats, while the strategists at headquarters thought of themselves as protectors of the throne. In a mostly futile effort to narrow that divide, managers of the local phone companies would be summoned to headquarters for a two-year stint, during which they would absorb (or more often ignore) the corporate culture before returning to the fold.

THE BEGINNING OF THE END

For many years, the Bell System existed as a fully self-contained world. By the 1960s, however, political and technological change had doomed the company's monopoly—and with it the old corporate culture of AT&T.

As competition crept into the telecommunications industry, Americans began to challenge AT&T's birthright. Did the country still need a phone monopoly? Why not open the market to competition?

The move from analog to digital represented a profound technological change. While traditional voice transmission used analog signals, new digital technology could simultaneously transmit voice and data. Solid-state electronic switching systems, microwave radio transmission (invented at Bell Labs), and satellite communication all eroded the value of the old network of copper wires—the original rationale for the government-sanctioned monopoly. As Judge Harold Greene, who presided over the breakup of the Bell System, declared: "It was a natural monopoly when it was wooden poles and copper wires. Once you could bypass it with microwaves, the monopoly could not survive."

An important part of this monopoly was the notion of end-to-end service. Because only Bell System equipment could be connected to the AT&T network, AT&T controlled every step of the transmission process. In 1968, though, the FCC's landmark Carterfone decision seriously compromised that control. For the first time, the law permitted companies to attach "foreign equipment" to the network of the Bell System. Answering machines, mobile phones, and similar devices manufactured by firms other than AT&T had legitimate commercial value now, because they could be attached to the Bell network. Suddenly, the Western Electric division of AT&T faced real competition.

That same year, MCI slipped into the long-distance market when the FCC approved its request to offer limited service between St. Louis and Chicago. As part of the ruling, MCI promised to stay out of the basic residential and business long-distance market, but in practice the decision allowed MCI to do just that. The effective deregulation of the U.S. telecommunications industry had begun.

In 1974 the Justice Department filed suit against AT&T, alleging "monopolization and a conspiracy to monopolize the supply of telecommunication service and equipment," a violation of the Sherman Act of 1890. The suit finally went to trial in 1981, and in January 1982 AT&T settled out of court. The old monopoly had become indefensible.

Even in the years after the government filed suit, the breakup of the Bell System had been literally inconceivable to the senior executives at AT&T. "In the beginning, the view among senior executives was that any change would go against God's will," recalls Block. "But eventually they came to feel that the endless antitrust suit was costing a fortune and sapping tremendous energy.

"The FCC was piling up new rules and regulations that encouraged our competitors and handicapped us. We also felt strongly—and in some cases wrongly—that if we had a chance to compete, why not?"

Initially, the government asked AT&T to sacrifice its manufacturing group and hold on to the local phone companies. AT&T executives waged a fierce campaign to keep Western Electric, and in the end the

Justice Department agreed. Ironically, the 1990s deregulation of the industry and the 1996 trivestiture completely reversed that original strategy; AT&T ended up selling the equipment business as it prepared to reenter local phone markets.

Back in the mid-1980s, though, the equipment group was the mechanical heart of the company. How could AT&T survive without it? For many business leaders, UCLA's Thomas Chandy points out, a basic pattern holds: the technology they grew up with defines their vision of the industry. Certainly this was the case at AT&T. "The AT&T mindset was, we must control the system, we must control the network. This meant they had to hang onto Western Electric and Bell Labs," Chandy states.

At the time, too, conventional wisdom supported that choice. Western Electric, with its cutting-edge technology, seemed destined to become a glamorous, fast-growing business. The local phone companies would remain as dull and stodgy as ever.

HUBRIS: "WE'LL KNOCK IBM OUT OF THE BOX"

There was one compensation for breaking up the Bell System, and for AT&T executives it held a powerful lure. As part of its settlement, the company could start selling computers, almost thirty years after a 1956 consent decree banned it from the business. Western Electric could be the sword to batter IBM, at that time the dominant force in computing.

Over the years, as the computer business had become one of the country's most important industries, AT&T executives followed its progress with a kind of yearning. While AT&T was still a monopoly, top management was busy fighting in the courts, in Congress, and with the FCC to preserve the company's basic business; it could not begin to contemplate competing in the computer industry. But after the 1982 breakup agreement, as experts declared that the telecommunications and computer industries were destined to converge, AT&T executives sat up and took notice.

After all, the executives reminded themselves, the digital switches that powered the phone network were themselves sophisticated computers. It was Bell Labs scientists who invented Unix, the computer programming language that became a widely respected standard among engineers and systems designers, to say nothing of the Bell Labs transistor that launched the digital revolution in the first place. Why shouldn't AT&T take the market by storm?

The answer might have been obvious. The company had no experience actually selling its technology. AT&T's insularity and grandiosity, sustained over years of dominating its core long distance business, made it impossible for its leaders to appreciate how ill-prepared they were to compete in this new industry. "In a sense it was worse than arrogance, it was innocence," says company spokesman Burke Stinson.

When AT&T was freed to start selling computers, its debut performance set the tone for its dismal future. Two months after the breakup of the Bell System, the company unveiled six models of personal computers, developed with Olivetti. None of them sold well.

Ken Matinale, a veteran computer programmer at AT&T until he retired in 1997, witnessed the self-delusion of senior management during this period. "They were good, solid phone guys," he says. "Gray suits, gray minds. They knew they had this thing Unix, whatever that was. They had the typical AT&T mentality: We'll go out and set the standards. and they failed miserably."

More than anyone, Bob Allen must assume the responsibility for this defeat. It was Allen who spent much of the late 1980s and early 1990s, first as head of the computer group (AT&T Information Systems) and later as president and chairman of the company, clinging to a fantasy of vanquishing the titans of the computer industry.

As AT&T's own Information Systems was flailing—outsiders estimated that it lost something like $2 billion between 1984 and 1991—Allen made the single worst judgment of his business career, pushing AT&T to acquire the NCR Corporation.

THE NCR DEBACLE

Like so many ill-fated corporate unions, AT&T's 1991 takeover of NCR began in a bidding war that spiraled out of control. After AT&T made its initial offer, the first hostile bid in the company's history, NCR chairman Charles Exley resisted. In an appearance before the AT&T board of directors, Exley made his case against the proposed deal by describing thirteen computer company mergers, all of them failures. "I told Bob Allen," Exley later recounted, "your outside advisers, the bankers and lawyers, aren't going to be around to pick up the pieces when it's all over. It's going to be you."

A clash of egos and a six-month proxy fight ensued. By the time a final deal was struck, AT&T's original offer of $6 billion had jumped to $7.5 billion—an enormous premium for a company that had earned just $369 million in 1991 on revenues of $3.6 billion. The difference between the first and the final offer, *Fortune* magazine noted at the time, was twice the market capitalization of Unisys, which was then a larger computer company. Exley himself left soon after the merger, with stock worth about $35 million. (When the *Wall Street Journal* tried to find him a few years later, he was sailing in the South Pacific.)

NCR, founded in 1884 when Dayton entrepreneur John Patterson bought the patent on the cash register, owned some attractive assets. It dominated the growing worldwide market for ATMs, made good money serving the banking and retailing sectors, and (unlike AT&T) had a strong presence outside North America. The real impetus behind the merger, however, was "convergence." Bob Allen had been infected by the virus of the time—the notion that telecommunications and computing technologies were converging, and that powerful synergies could be realized by companies that combined them. In theory, AT&T would join NCR's data networks with AT&T's own communications systems, and somehow the whole would be greater than the sum of its parts.

By 1990, though, NCR was widely regarded as an also-ran in the computer industry. Everyone knew that, including Bob Allen. Ken Matinale recalls attending a company briefing when executive vice president Robert Kavner, a strong advocate of the merger, came to rally Wall Street financial analysts behind the deal. "If you're going to buy a computer company," Kavner was asked, "why do you want to be number five?" There was no good answer.

"NCR was past its prime. But somehow we failed to notice this," says one AT&T manager.

Once the deal was done, basic business problems were exacerbated by AT&T's overbearing pride. No action had greater symbolic value than AT&T's decision to erase the NCR logo and rename the computer division "AT&T Global Information Solutions." AT&T executives thought their own brand name was the greater asset. This judgment proved cavalier and foolish, and it had the predictable effect of alienating many NCR veterans.

A clash of corporate cultures did not in itself doom the merger, but it proved a constant distraction. To an outsider, AT&T and NCR might have seemed rather similar: two old-line American companies with slow-moving bureaucracies. Yet NCR, it soon became clear, was considerably more hierarchical. The differences were intensified by the fact that Jerre Stead, the executive brought in to run the computer group in 1993, had only recently joined AT&T.

A former Honeywell executive and electronics industry veteran, Stead was far more freewheeling than the typical product of the AT&T culture, and he determined that NCR's straitlaced troops should loosen up. In one of his trademark cardigan sweaters, he proclaimed that he wasn't anyone's boss; instead, he was the "head coach." Head coaches could still give orders, of course, and one of Stead's memorable fiats decreed that no manager could hide behind closed doors. All office doors, he declared, must be replaced with glass. When NCR president R. Elton White balked, he returned to his office one afternoon to find that his wooden door had disappeared.

Some NCR staffers saw Stead as more of a rabble-rouser than a true corporate leader. "He seemed like a preacher," says John Geary, an NCR sales veteran who retired in 1994 as New York manager in charge of ATMs. "It was as if he had his religion and he was determined to bring it to everyone in the company."

For a year or so, losses at the new Global Information Solutions could be managed (or at least ignored), and Bob Allen could believe that his latest savior—he named a total of ten computer heads in eleven years—would redeem his costly vision. By 1994, though, the division began to unravel; a year later, it was in tatters. During 1995 alone, the group reported operating losses of $720 million. When the final numbers were tallied, AT&T admitted that it had pumped $3.3 billion into the division in an effort to cover those losses and salvage the ill-fated acquisition of NCR.

The drain on the energy and spirit of senior management was as debilitating, in its way, as the appalling financial statements. To see the losses mount was to see the plainest proof that Bob Allen's grand corporate vision of converging telecommunications and computer technologies was, in the end, a mirage.

Even if AT&T's foray into computers had not been such a spectacular fiasco, the fundamental integration that was at the core of AT&T since the nineteenth century—the union between telecommunications equipment and service—was becoming untenable. This was not Bob Allen's fault, but it became his problem. In an increasingly deregulated global market, AT&T's equipment group found it increasingly difficult to sell to phone companies, such as Canada's Northern Telcom and the baby Bells. The phone companies saw no reason to buy equipment from one division of AT&T when they either did or would compete with AT&T in selling phone service. Deregulation of the U.S. industry seemed inevitable (and, in fact, the long-awaited legislation was enacted in 1996). Bob Allen bowed to this inevitability when he announced the trivestiture of AT&T and the accompanying layoffs.

DOWNSIZING

The larger story of downsizing at AT&T, though, goes back to the breakup of the Bell System. In November 1983, a few months before the actual divestiture, the company offered early retirement deals to 13,000 employees. No one was actually fired; instead, called into an executive's office, an employee would be told that perhaps it was time to leave. There was widespread suspicion that the buyout offers would only become less generous as time passed (and they did).

All told, between 1984 and 1995, about 120,000 people disappeared from the company payrolls. Some of these departures were voluntary, but an increasingly visible number were not.

Bob Allen orchestrated AT&T's first major involuntary downsizing in 1985, when the Information Systems group (the computer division) announced plans to cut nearly 25,000 jobs. Though a good number of the announced job cuts failed to materialize because employees managed to find other jobs within the company, layoffs continued through the 1980s. "These were the early days of downsizing in the U.S., and getting fired was still a stigma then," says one manager. "It hit people hard." The strain of the downsizing pushed one supervisor of security guards over the edge. He shot himself in the middle of the night; his body was discovered in the executive suite at company headquarters the next morning.

What distinguished the layoffs of the 1980s and 1990s was that they targeted white-collar workers; AT&T had been laying off factory workers and eliminating operator jobs for years. The pace quickened as changes in technology made many blue-collar positions obsolete. In 1984, for example, AT&T employed 44,000 operators; by the start of 1994 their ranks had fallen to about 15,000. By 1996 only 8,000 operators worked for AT&T, and many of those jobs will probably be gone by the end of the decade.

DOWNSIZING FOR THE PEOPLE

Many companies resort to Orwellian language to dull the impact of a layoff. The attempt is always transparent, but somehow the vocabulary endures. At AT&T, "you're accepted for the package" means you're fired. "You're involuntarily separated" means you're fired. "Your job won't be there going forward" means you're fired.

Back in the spring of 1995, long before AT&T's downsizing became front-page news, AT&T public-relations man Burke Stinson spoke openly about these sorry euphemisms. "If I tell you it's downsizing, you won't think people are getting fired. Sometimes executives allow consultants to pull the wool over their eyes," he said, "as if the masses, the employees, won't see right through it. Top executives who know the value of straightforward communication can take a simple concept— shutting a factory, reducing jobs—and call it something else: 're-engineering,' or worse, 'serving our customers better.' It's just silly. You have much greater credibility when you speak plain English."

Downsizing at AT&T is a peculiar process. In some respects it is more humane than it is at other companies, but it can also be more unsettling. At other firms, when employees are laid off, they're soon gone. At AT&T, targeted employees are first placed "at risk" and "made available for reassignment"; their job becomes "surplus."

Then an oddly choreographed ritual begins, as employees frantically try to find a new job within the company. They ask their boss to curry favor with colleagues, they call upon any contacts or connections they have made. The human resources department has no responsibility to help them here, so employees work fast. If they find another position within sixty days, they are saved; if not, they are unemployed.

The system has its defenders. Why shouldn't an employee laid off in Chicago save his job by filling an opening in a Florida office? Indeed, at AT&T this frequently happens. On average, the company says, more than half of all vulnerable employees find a new job within the company before the sixty-day clock stops ticking.

DOWNSIZING FOR THE VICE PRESIDENTS

Senior executives are spared such public humiliation. They are never declared to be "at risk," nor do they search for cubicle space at company resource centers; AT&T finds them an out-of-the-way office along a quiet corridor. But while the vice presidents are handled one by one, and their severance packages are considerably more generous than those of their subordinates, they still feel their own shame. As Andrea McGregor, a manager in the human resources department puts it, "They get to the same place."

Jack Murphy's story is representative. (His name and certain identifying details have been changed.) Jack began his AT&T career as a salesman for New York Telephone in 1971. His father-in-law, who would retire from the company after thirty-five years, arranged for the initial interview. By the early 1980s Jack was heading up a small sales office; after being twice named the top branch manager in the United States, he was promoted to vice president before the decade was over.

Jack made it through two restructurings, and in 1993 his boss handed him what he said was the largest bonus he had ever delivered. His total compensation that year was close to $300,000—but a few months after he received it, a third restructuring claimed his job.

"Coming off my success in 1992, I wasn't worried," Jack says. "What a mistake that was!" He cut a deal with his boss to take another position in the company, a step below the vice-presidential level, where he could hang on for two more years. That way he could leave AT&T in 1995, when his pension would include lifetime medical insurance. "When 1995 comes around, you're going to retire, right? You're not going to come to me looking for a job?" his boss asked. Jack agreed, and they shook hands on the deal.

"So," Jack says, "when the 1995 downsizing package was announced I got a call from our human resources people. They said, 'You're leaving, right?' I said, 'Don't get nervous. I'll honor my commitment, I'll shrink into the woodwork, and off I'll go. And by the way, since I was going to leave anyway, thank you for the severance package.'"

THE 40,000 LAYOFFS THAT WEREN'T

Despite its years of downsizing, AT&T retained much of its reputation as a "good" employer. That was eviscerated overnight on January 2, 1996, with one number: 40,000.

"40,000 Employees Laid Off at AT&T," the next day's headlines read, and for months afterward the media repeated the number as a perfect symbol of the demise of the safe job.

But AT&T planned to cut 40,000 jobs, not 40,000 people; some employees would lose one job, change corridors, and find another. The layoff proclamation proved to be ugly posturing by a company that was trying to look tough to please Wall Street. Ultimately, considerably less than 40,000 jobs were cut in 1996.

When the downsizing was unveiled, though, such a denouement seemed impossible. AT&T announced that about 40,000 jobs would vanish in the next three years, with 70 percent of them (28,000 jobs) disappearing within twelve months. The strategy was set, and its execution would be swift. No one could accuse AT&T chairman Bob Allen of timidity; no one could argue that he was clinging to AT&T's ancient heritage of lifetime employment.

To make certain of this last point AT&T declared—almost boasted—that about three-fourths of the 40,000 lost jobs would be "involuntary" cuts. In other words, the targeted employee would very much want to hang on. Making such a projection was a change for AT&T, as everyone inside the company knew. It seemed a shameless exercise in looking "lean and mean" for Wall Street (the dreary cliché still had currency in Basking Ridge).

"There was a macho [feeling] among some executives," AT&T's Stinson later admitted, "a desire to show that we're not soft in the belly."

"When I heard the number 30,000," Stinson recalled, "I thought it seemed high, given the track record employees have for finding jobs elsewhere in the company. Will this number of people really leave the payroll? I asked that question. Yes, they said. That was the answer every time."

The bluster quickly faded. AT&T's downsizing came less than two months before the company's proxy statement reported Allen's record compensation package: salary and bonus of $2.7 million, and a whopping 750,000 stock options with a present value of $11 million. The timing was appalling, and Allen inevitably appeared as the perfect symbol of corporate greed. In a scathing *Newsweek* cover story, the chairman's mug-shot photo was featured as one of several "corporate killers."

A year later, as it happened, AT&T's stock had plummeted and Allen's options were worthless. Poetic justice, perhaps.

Certainly the downsizing—its messiness as much as the company's seeming callousness—had caused incalculable damage to the value of the AT&T brand name, which the company spends about $500 million a year to promote.

If, as seems likely, AT&T's 1996 downsizing becomes a business school case study, what will be the moral of the story? Executive vice president Hal Burlingame, the head of the human resources department and one of the top officers of AT&T, considered the question in the summer of 1996, when the company was long gone from the headlines. His convoluted, clumsy response seemed to reflect the bureaucracy he had served for thirty-four years:

We've had a decade plus of changing the business and getting to the place it could change from a monopoly into a competitive business. Almost from the breakup of the Bell System, if you took a snapshot of any three-year period, you'd find that we adjusted the traditional work force by something approaching the number we in 1996 adjusted this work force by, during this three-year period. So there has been this whole series of changes. This one was slightly accelerated because we had broken up the company and that caused us to look very differently at our staffs and connective tissues. . . .

So the lessons of it are, it was part of a long-term change process in an industry that had been in a monopoly environment and changed to a competitive environment. And now, one more time, it was taking a kind of step-function change in its organization to get ready to go separately in three distinct markets.

Burke Stinson was, characteristically, more forthcoming: "When a company projects a gloomy employment picture, the coverage is going to be widespread. Normally, it peters out. What moved the downsizing story, from a PR perspective, were three things. First, obviously, the 40,000; it's a big number. Then, Allen's compensation. Then, within weeks we said that the 30,000 [the share of the job cuts that would be involuntary] will probably drop to 18,000."

This last fact became known in an embarrassingly haphazard manner. The new layoff projection first appeared in the media when Bob Allen slipped it into a speech he made in Florida. The Los Angeles Times covered the speech and included the number; the Associated Press then picked up the newspaper's story. There the matter might have rested. But several weeks later, AT&T took out full-page ads in newspapers across the country that asked companies to hire its downsized workers. Many viewed the ad as a crude attempt to refurbish the public image of the company ("Look, we're not as heartless as we've been made out to be").

"So reporters started calling us," Stinson recalled. "And they asked us, 'What's the story?' And we said, 'Well, it looks like the 30,000 involuntary layoffs will actually be 18,000.' [As a result] our credibility was strained with the media and, no less important, with our own people."

BOB ALLEN'S LEGACY

Those who followed Bob Allen's career never imagined that he was destined for either the fame or the notoriety he inspired as chairman of AT&T. To many he was a capable, but unexceptional executive; temperamentally aloof, he fit no one's definition of a natural leader.

Allen might never have gotten the top job at AT&T if his predecessor, James Olson, had not suddenly died only two years into his tenure. What happened to Allen seems a textbook case of corner-office arrogance. When times were good and the press was sympathetic, it almost seemed he could do no wrong. The man who came of age in the stodgy Bell System was suddenly thrust into a leading role in one of the nation's most important industries.

Allen answered to an extremely loyal board of directors. They received stinging criticism for authorizing Allen's controversial 1996 compensation, as well as for the way they handled the search for a new president. John Walter, the former chief executive of R.R. Donnelly, got the job but kept it for only nine months before he walked off with a $26 million farewell package, which softened the sting of AT&T board member Walter Elisha's crude outburst that John Walter had lacked the "intellectual leadership" to lead AT&T. Elisha himself belonged to a board which *Business Week,* in the fall of 1996, ranked as the sixth worst in the U.S.

"Bob Allen is like an epic figure who has had endless praise," said one AT&T manager not long after the debacle of the 40,000. "Then one morning he arises to find nothing but trouble at the door. He's baby-skinned, you see. He's never taken a punch this hard. He worries about his place in history. Finally he says to himself, 'Son of a bitch! I'm going to be remembered for this!'"

WHAT SURVIVES OF THE OLD SERVICE CULTURE?

As his retirement loomed, Allen made a last-ditch attempt to salvage his reputation. In the spring of 1997, he began discussing a possible $50 billion merger with SBC, a company that itself combined the assets of two baby Bells—Southwestern Bell and Pacific Telesis. The *Wall Street Journal* broke the news of the talks, and soon the proposed combination was challenged—quite reasonably—as potentially anti-competitive. Among its critics was the outgoing head of the FCC, Reed Hunt. Allen, who never formally admitted meeting with SBC, nonetheless publicly defended the idea of such a merger. (He also undercut the status of president John Walter, his putative heir apparent, who had reportedly been kept out of the important meetings with SBC.) In the end, the proposed deal unraveled and AT&T's board took charge of the search for Allen's successor. Allen had reportedly hoped that his confidant, vice chairman John Zeglis, could get the job, but he was rebuffed when Michael Armstrong, the Hughes CEO, took charge.

As Allen—surely the last of the Bell System men to lead AT&T—stepped off the stage, the question was unavoidable: Will AT&T one day be remembered as a historic American company that somehow lost its way? To avoid this fate, AT&T must recreate its identity. AT&T, *the* phone company for more than a hundred years, must now prove that it is more than just another phone company.

The corporation still claims an extraordinary base of 90 million American customers. Most of all, it owns one of the great American brand names. The value of that asset cannot be measured, but there is no doubt that it has eroded badly in the past few years.

To reaffirm the power of its logo, AT&T must reconnect with its old corporate culture of customer service. To the extent that telecommunications offerings seem basically indistinguishable to most consumers, good service can define the difference between brands. Much of this old culture has vanished, but the battle to resurrect it is being waged—as it must be—on the company's front lines, by men like Bob Cain and by women like Flo Kiesel, Cookie Alexander, and Andrea Green.

Bob Cain is an unassuming man who has worked for AT&T for thirty-one of his fifty-one years. Today he runs three of AT&T's eleven customer care centers; his Pittsburgh center handles business customers whose monthly AT&T bill is $5,000 or less. If a customer needs any service—a billing adjustment, a maintenance call, product information—

he or she can now, for the first time, make a single call to AT&T. The company calls this one-stop shopping "total customer care," hoping it will prove a competitive advantage.

Staffing the phone lines are two hundred workers—about half of them displaced telephone operators, mostly from AT&T's Grant Street international operator office just across the Monongahela River. A Pittsburgh native, Bob opened the Grant Street center back in 1969, when calling overseas was still exotic and expensive. More than twenty-five years later, he helped many of the Grant Street staff find a new livelihood.

One of them was Flo Kiesel. Flo worked as an operator until her job was eliminated in 1994; she joined Bob's Pittsburgh operation when it opened one year later. "You're working for it, but it's good money, eighteen dollars an hour," says Flo, the mother of two young children. "Not too many people out there make it."

Cookie Alexander, a Pittsburgh native who started working as an operator in 1973, had enough seniority to avoid the downsizing of the Grant Street office. "But I was feeling stale," she recalls, and in the back of her mind was the looming obsolescence of the operator's job. She volunteered to join the customer care center.

Bob's rescue mission was not an act of altruism. By 1993, when it was clear that the old operator center would be decimated (the downsizing actually struck the following year) Bob knew that he himself would have to find a new job at AT&T. A well-regarded veteran, he felt confident that he would find something. But Bob very much wanted to stay in Pittsburgh, and that might have proved a problem.

To find a solution, he did what every corporate survivor learns to do—he worked the phones. "I called everyone I knew in the company," Bob recalls. "We have hardworking, skilled people here, I told them; we have good, inexpensive office space. Think of us if you're looking to start up a new operation."

After the 1994 downsizing, the payroll of the Grant Street operation fell from 700 to 350 workers. By this time, AT&T management had launched its "one-stop shopping" strategy and planned to open a service center for business customers. In February 1995, one of his many contacts told Bob to start looking for office space. The definitive call approving a lease came two months later.

"Thank you for calling AT&T Customer Care center. This is Andrea Green, how may I help you?"

This is hard work. Call after call, complaint after query, service representatives sit in front of a computer screen—switching among fifteen different software systems, sustaining a steady rhythm as they click along. They are expected to handle one call every seven or eight minutes, and their response time is tracked by computer.

The system's endless acronyms can be mystifying.

"Plan Identification required—what does that mean?" Andrea asks a colleague as she struggles to enter the appropriate data.

"Try the MBN number. That code should get you on an SBA . . . so do a Model T."

"The PTSS?"

"That's the station number."

"But how do I code it?"

"Oh, so it's optimization, IN8S . . . ."

As the calls back up, the computer keeps track of her every move.

Andrea and her colleagues work on an invisible assembly line. They are, in many ways, the steelworkers of the 1990s. Their fingernails are clean, but this can still be grueling, numbing labor. Like the steelworkers whose spirit still lingers in this city, these women share a fundamental work ethic: they make a good wage, but they earn it.

In a hierarchical company like AT&T, one rises through the ranks or falls through the cracks. Lost ground is rarely regained. Bob Cain, however, became a rare exception to that rule.

Like many of his generation, Bob arrived at AT&T without a college degree. In 1965, just out of technical school, he took a job as a communications technician in the Long Lines division, where he installed and repaired phone lines. Then from late 1967 to early 1969 he served in Vietnam, in communications support; he saw a lot of combat.

Back at AT&T, Bob worked in technical operations through the 1970s, and then in sales and project management through the 1980s. Along the way, he earned a bachelor's degree from Robert Morris College in Pittsburgh.

Bob was a third-level manager in 1989 when he volunteered to take a demotion. He was working in Virginia then, and when he learned that his mother-in-law in Pittsburgh had been diagnosed with terminal cancer, Bob and his wife were determined to move back home. Since there were no third-level manager jobs available, Bob accepted a second-level assignment. "This was a family decision," he says, "and we never once regretted it."

Not long after his successful launch of the Pittsburgh center, AT&T returned to Bob the title he had given up seven years before.

Not every boss would inspire such a response, but the Pittsburgh staffers cheered Bob's promotion. They saw it as one small sign that respect for the company's culture and heritage—and the operators who helped build it—was not yet extinct at AT&T.

MOVING ON

Barbara David is a self-sufficient, self-possessed salesperson. Larry Nagel is a blunt-speaking, rumpled-looking engineer who likes to "add things up and see what you get." Both believed that their professional identity was critical to their sense of self. In the wake of the downsizing, they moved on, and moved fast. Abandoning any lingering attachment to the old community of AT&T, they made a new place for themselves in the corporate world. They do not call it home.

4   BARBARA DAVID

Barbara was six years old when she taught herself how to swim.

Her mother had just died, suddenly, at the age of thirty-nine. Her two brothers (aged thirteen and fifteen) were remote figures, and her father, a traveling salesman, was on the road from Monday morning to Friday night.

Barbara was on her own. It was the middle of June, the start of a long summer. She and her brothers were in northern Wisconsin, living with an aunt while their father was back in Illinois arranging to sell the family house. The boys were tossing a ball on a rolling lawn near a lake when their little sister fell into the deep, cold water. Somehow she started to swim. What Barbara vividly remembers, all these years later, is not fear or panic, but simply an amazing sense of triumph.

This lonely strength, an independence born of isolation, defines her life story. Her fortitude comes at an emotional cost, but it also gives Barbara a resiliency that has carried her through the inescapable setbacks of her business career.

When Barbara was laid off from her job as a sales account executive at AT&T during the downsizing of 1995–96, she held her head above water and kept on moving. "I knew that I couldn't look back," she says. Unemployed for less than three months, she found a better job at a smaller and, she feels, kinder company. She did it on her own.

Tall and slim, with short blonde hair framing a fine-featured face, Barbara is an attractive woman. At the age of forty-two, she selects her clothes carefully and well—sweater dresses during the week, denim vests and jeans on weekends, adorned sometimes by dangling earrings and silk scarves. Her style reflects her temperament: clean, straight, no nonsense.

As a salesperson, she does her homework, listens well, and makes her pitch plainly and directly. She envies colleagues who have a light touch and have mastered "the gift of gab"—a talent that has always eluded her.

When she was twenty-three and single, when she married at thirty-four, and now that she is divorced and living alone, Barbara has always been a capable, self-sufficient professional. When she lost her job, she knew she would ultimately prevail. Her conviction was born from the experience of a difficult life.

———————

Barbara's parents married in a Technicolor image of the 1940s. They met on a midnight flight from Tulsa to Los Angeles, the night the Japanese bombed Pearl Harbor. Virginia, a beautiful young airline stewardess, was not scheduled to be on this particular flight, but she boarded at the last minute. Not many passengers were traveling at this late hour, so she spent much of the flight talking to Henry, a young fighter pilot who had caught her eye. Before the plane landed he asked her out on a date. A few months later, they married.

A decorated flier during World War II, Henry returned home in 1945. Less than a year later their first child, David, was born; two years after that, Jim arrived. Henry remembers the family's early years as happy and close, and he has especially sweet memories of playing outside with his boys.

After a brief stint as a drugstore manager, Henry realized that he had something in common with his own father, a soft drink salesman—he would never be able to tolerate the confinement of an office job. And so Henry began a forty-year career on the road selling pharmaceuticals.

Left at home all week with two young children, Virginia's life slowly came undone. She compulsively overate, eventually to the point of obesity, and spent most of the day asleep in bed. After Barbara was born, her psychological dislocation became more and more incapacitating. She loved her children, but could barely take care of them. "The truth is," says her son Jim, "that even when we had a mother we didn't have a mother."

Barbara's father only dimly understood how troubled his wife had become. "Looking back," he says, "I can see that she needed professional help, but she never did get it." Once he brought his wife to the Mayo Clinic for a psychiatric consultation, but nothing ever came of it.

When Virginia developed dangerously high blood pressure, a family doctor sent her to a Chicago hospital for observation. It was there, on Father's Day in 1960, that she died of a heart attack; an autopsy revealed that her coronary arteries were 90 percent blocked.

"These things happen," Barbara's father told his children in the kitchen the next morning. Dave and Jim burst into tears, but Barbara was numb. She showed no emotion at all.

"Do you understand what I'm telling you?" her father softly asked.

"Yes, you're telling me that Mommy died."

Her father thought it odd that Barbara never once broke down and cried. Instead, she made a silent retreat into herself. Something very powerful had been set in motion, and it would not be reversed.

For the first months after his wife's death, Henry's employer gave him an office job, and he was able to spend more time with his family. Through the summer and fall, he took Barbara for long rides in the country, singing children's songs as they drove along. They both have vivid memories of this time together.

Within a year, though, Henry was back on the road. Aunt Gladys, a stern German woman in her sixties, was the first in a series of female caretakers who did what they could to help raise Barbara and her brothers. No one dared to disobey her.

Henry worked for the same company for many years, but he was relocated many times, and Barbara ended up at seven different schools before she went to college. "We were always moving. That was the fact and the feeling of my childhood," she says.

Several women—aunts on both sides of her family—came into Barbara's life, but none of them became a maternal figure. Between the ages of eight and eleven, Barbara spent summers with an aunt and uncle in Philadelphia's Main Line, where she observed for the first time the power of money. Her uncle Tim was a smart, successful lawyer; her aunt Joan was a good-looking, formidable woman. "She was a queen," Barbara says, recalling the awe and terror this particular aunt inspired in her. "She was beautiful, domineering and utterly intimidating." Some complicated feelings endure: "I admired her greatly," Barbara says now, "and I still do."

In the parlor one afternoon when Barbara was eleven, her aunt looked up from the magazine she was reading. "Do you know anything about menstruation?" she asked. Not waiting for a response, she added, "Once a month you bleed."

Later that afternoon, Joan went to the library and brought her niece a handful of books on the subject. Barbara was grateful for the chance to read them quietly in the privacy of her room. "Everyone was good to me, in their own way," she says. "They asked themselves, what are we going to do about Barbara? How will she be raised?"

———————————

Barbara never complained—not to her father, not to her aunts, and not to herself. She did what she was told. "There was no whining, no discussion, no nasty looks," her father says. During these years, Henry did not give much thought to his children's emotional state, or his own. It was all he could do to keep himself moving from client to client, trying to close the next sale.

At the age of seventy-seven, as he considers the course of his daughter's childhood, Henry now realizes that Barbara was on her own much more than he knew at the time. He lived the ordinary life of a company salesman, but his circumstances were anything but ordinary, and his family paid a price. "I was gone from Monday to Friday, and that's no way to have a family. Do I feel that I abandoned them? Yes, I do."

For her first year in high school, her father chose a Pennsylvania boarding school. On his salary the tuition was not insignificant, but he knew that Barbara needed stability after being shuttled around so many times.

When Barbara arrived at Eden Hall, a Catholic girls' school outside Philadelphia, her life changed for the better. The school was housed in an old brick building, full of rich, dark wood and a majestic staircase that Barbara thought was beautiful. And for a traditional girls' school of the time, Eden Hall was unusually open and genuinely collegial. Twenty-five years after Barbara first saw the Eden Hall campus, the mention of its name entirely transforms her face. "It was warm and supportive and caring," she says—everything that had been absent from her life for so long.

At Eden Hall an obedient, shy child transformed herself into a spirited young woman. But Barbara had spent just two semesters there when the school, facing financial difficulty, decided to close. "Finally I had found a place where I was happy," Barbara says. "It would have made such a difference in my life if I had been able to stay."

At nearly the same time, her father remarried. Barbara would eventually grow quite fond of Lynn, her stepmother, who was twenty years younger than Henry and only fifteen years older than she was. At this point in her adolescence, though, the last thing Barbara wanted to do was move to Missouri to live with them. Her father agreed that she could go to a new boarding school on the East Coast. She chose Marymount Academy, in upstate New York, where some of her Eden Hall friends were headed. There Barbara met a day student, Jean, who would become a lifelong friend; together they sang in the glee club and cheered on the one rebel nun in the strict Catholic school.

Barbara had always done what was expected of her, but when it came time for college, she defied her father. He wanted her to go to school in Missouri and become a nurse or a secretary; tuition outside the state would cost three times as much, and Henry had already spent a considerable sum on Barbara's education. "Why not find a good school right here?" he asked his daughter.

"That's not what I want to do," Barbara told him. "I want to stay on the East Coast. Finally, I've made some friends, and I don't want to lose them."

"If you insist on this," her father told her, "you'll be on your own."

"That's fine," Barbara said. She was disappointed, but there was no rancor in her voice. She knew very well what it meant to be on her own.

Barbara won a scholarship, took out a student loan, worked odd jobs, and used Social Security survivor benefits that she received upon her mother's death to pay her own way through college. In 1976 she graduated *magna cum laude* from the University of Bridgeport with a bachelor's degree in psychology.

"I had thought she'd come around and move back to Missouri," her father says. "But she had made up her mind that she was going to do this, come hell or high water. I admire her for that."

Her brother Jim also finds cause for admiration, which he expresses in his own blunt fashion: "Barbara learned early on how to take care of herself. She's a tougher piece of leather than my dad ever knew."

After she graduated, a lifelong love of horses inspired Barbara to take a job at a race track where she took the animals for long, slow walks to cool down after a run. It was hard, dangerous work—and Barbara, it turned out, had no affinity for it. "Race horses are magnificent, schizoid animals," she says, "and they instinctively smell fear."

Barbara was hopeful about her future when she received tragic news: her brother Dave had killed himself. While he was visiting Jim, their brother and his best friend, Dave went into an empty room, put a gun to his head, and pulled the trigger; Jim found the body. Dave was thirty-one years old, and he left behind a wife and two young daughters. There was no note.

What deep despair compelled Dave to take his own life, no one could begin to fathom. He had lost his job and gambled away most of his money, his marriage was foundering, and a stomach ulcer left him in considerable pain. Jim believes that his brother had also begun to abuse drugs in his final months.

Barbara and her family comforted each other as best they could, but they were scattered across the country and no one really knew where to begin. Year after year, on the anniversary of Dave's death, Barbara still feels flooded by a sense of loss.

_____

Barbara's business career began at a small New York City executive search firm that specialized in placing women in sales and marketing positions; for several years she worked there as a career counselor. In the late 1970s women were just beginning to enter the workforce in dramatic numbers, and Barbara found it gratifying to help her female clients, many of them middle-aged schoolteachers who were looking for a second career.

After a few years, she took a job in the marketing department of the New York Stock Exchange. Two years later, she was promoted to a high-profile position as executive assistant to the chairman. In that role she helped develop the long-term strategy for the exchange and served as a liaison between member firms and the executive staff.

Her most public performance (and, for Barbara, her most rewarding) came in 1979, when the exchange embarked upon a major overhaul of its technology—essentially deciding to computerize the entire trading-room floor over the course of several weeks. Among the relics to be abandoned were the old oak and brass trading posts that had stood on the floor since 1929.

Barbara has an affection for historic artifacts (in her apartment she keeps a 1930s cash register and a piece of the 1920s Big Board) and she was determined to save the posts from the scrap heap. With a $10,000 stipend from the exchange, she quickly rounded up a group of brokerage firms who helped her find sponsors. Each one paid about $35,000 and together they arranged the transfer of the posts to the Smithsonian, Harvard Business School, and a handful of other institutions.

In 1984, approaching her thirtieth birthday, Barbara did something uncharacteristically impulsive. She quit her job and put herself on a plane to California, planning to look for work in a burgeoning field that had captured her imagination: interactive technology. During the preceding several years, Barbara had become a student of this new technology; she was particularly drawn to the notion of "fantasy rooms," precursors of what are now called virtual-reality games. She was haunted by the prospect of living out a fantasy in a semi-real state. What would it actually feel like to be a jockey? Often she thought of her brother in the last weeks of his life. What if Dave had someplace like that to go when he was feeling so desperate?

In California, Barbara interviewed with George Lucas's company and a handful of Silicon Valley firms that were developing this new technology. Still, her enthusiasm could not compensate for her lack of experience or credentials, and she did not manage to find a job. After working in her brother's small limousine business for several months, she decided to return to New York.

On the flight home, she came upon a magazine article that described a new master's program in interactive telecommunications at New York University. "That's it!" she said to herself. "That's what I've been looking for!" She was accepted into the graduate school a few months later. This time, her father offered to help with the tuition, and Barbara arranged part-time work as a marketing consultant.

One morning when a cash deposit at her bank's ATM machine failed to register in her checking account, she realized that she had found a subject for her master's thesis. They were not fantasy rooms or virtual-reality games, but clearly ATMs had become the central interactive technology used by millions of Americans. "When you think about it," Barbara says, "in their early days, ATMs had to elicit trust. It's one thing to take cash from an ATM, and it's another thing to have faith that a deposited check will not disappear into a black void."

And so she wrote a research paper entitled, "The ATM as Witness," which analyzed consumer attitudes toward this new technology. A year later, the paper was published as a marketing monograph by a financial trade association.

Making use of her expertise in ATMs, Barbara applied for jobs at the two companies that dominated the ATM business, and still do— NCR, which has the leading position in the global market, and Diebold, the number one company in the United States. She signed on with NCR as an account manager handling ATM sales. It was 1989, three years before the Dayton-based company was acquired by AT&T in a doomed corporate merger.

In February 1989, a few months before she started working at NCR, Barbara married Mort, a man with whom she had been involved on and off for a decade.

Mort had appeared as the romantic figure of her imagination: dark, suave, intriguing. When they first met, Barbara was twenty-four and Mort was forty-seven, the divorced father of three grown children and something of a ladies' man. Barbara and Mort both loved to cook (they shared a special weakness for chocolate) and they traveled well together. On the surface they seemed a good match, yet the emotional equation between them was never quite in balance.

Over the years, they battled in a familiar pas de deux: when one of them was ready to make a commitment, the other was flying out the door. After they had known each other for five years, Mort proposed. At that moment, at the age of fifty-one, he was prepared to have more children. Barbara turned him down. She didn't trust that the relationship could last.

When they did finally marry seven years later, it was with two significant caveats. Mort asked Barbara to sign a prenuptial agreement. It said, essentially, that she could have no claim on his assets, which included a Manhattan co-op and his market research firm. "I gave my first wife everything when we got divorced," Mort says, "and I couldn't go through that again." Barbara signed.

Mort was fifty-eight when they married and no longer interested in having more children. Barbara told him that she accepted his decision, but as she got older and several of her close friends became pregnant, she yearned for a baby. Mort remained adamantly opposed to the idea. As often happens, this tension became a proxy for all the other strains in their relationship. One day, Mort asked his wife for a divorce: they had been married for just three years.

Barbara began looking for a place to live after Thanksgiving, at the start of the holiday season. "To see people's homes, to catch a glimpse of their lives was painful for me," Barbara recalls. For the first months of their separation, Mort helped Barbara settle into her new apartment; he bought her some nice furniture, painted the walls, and put up shelves. "That was the generous side of Mort," Barbara says. But finally he made it a cold parting. On the strength of their prenuptial agreement, he insisted on a tough financial settlement. Years later he says, defensively, that he did the best he could. "When we got divorced, my business was not doing well. I simply did not have the money."

"Mort was very businesslike and pragmatic about the divorce," says Jean, Barbara's old friend. "Maybe he never had as much at stake, emotionally. I might have worried that Barbara would never get him out of her system. But he gave her a very good reason to clean house and move on."

Loneliness engulfed her. "I was devastated by the breakup," she says. "It tore me apart." Whatever the problems in her marriage, her life with Mort had given Barbara her only real home. She thought back on their long relationship and wondered if they had ever shared a real intimacy.

More than any other trauma, the divorce threatened Barbara's sense of self. She found solace in her friends and family, and the day-to-day demands of her job. Her work gave her life meaning, of that she was sure. Yet suddenly it all seemed so hollow.

Keep moving. That is what Barbara said to herself, what she had always said to herself in the face of profound anxiety. She said it without words when she was a little girl and her mother died, she had said it in the wake of her brother's suicide, and she would say it later, too.

———————

To be in sales is to be in constant motion, answering beeping pagers and writing proposals on laptops at thirty thousand feet. There is also the motion of the job itself, the constant need to look ahead to the next presentation, to anticipate the problem that could sabotage the deal.

Based in New York City, Barbara joined the sales team that served the financial services industry, selling ATMs to banks and retailers. Success in sales is measured in raw numbers, and Barbara made or surpassed her quota most years. She earned the plaudits that came with the territory: district sales leader for ATMs for two years, customer focus team award for one year.

At AT&T, clients and bosses came to appreciate her unusual dedication. When an ATM shipment was delayed somewhere between a plant in Scotland and a dock in downtown Manhattan, Barbara tracked its journey literally from port to port. "Barbara was unusually conscientious," recalls the banker who had placed the order and whose credibility was on the line. "Most account executives would tell you, 'Well, your order is on a ship someplace, we'll let you know when it comes in.'"

Like any good account executive, Barbara recognized the important client who could make her name; in her case, it was a New York City bank. After receiving an assignment to become the manager of the account in 1991, she went on to sell the institution a record number of ATMs.

This was the crucial client relationship of her AT&T career, and Barbara's experience with this particular bank is an emblematic story of the vagaries and coldness of the corporate world. When things were going well—machines were being sold and installed, the client was happy, the boss was happy—Barbara was secure. When her relationship with the bank began to fray, however, there would be no credit for past performance, no accumulated goodwill on which to draw. Business is business.

The good times lasted three years—from 1991 to 1994, a period that coincided with AT&T's takeover and absorption of the NCR corporation. During this time, and as she worked on smaller accounts as well, Barbara collected several awards. Her clients expressed their appreciation in the generic corporate clichés: "Barbara goes the extra mile," "When she makes a deal, it's a win-win situation," "She gets the job done"—even, that important bank would attest, in the midst of a torrential storm.

This drama began with a commonplace occurrence, a banking acquisition. Barbara's client announced the takeover of another New York bank in the middle of the summer. "We'll replace their ATMs with ours some time between Columbus Day and New Year's Eve," the bankers informed Barbara and her colleagues. "The work must be completed by the end of the year, you understand."

This did not give Barbara and her colleagues much time. Still, it was a major assignment, which meant that their response was already scripted: "Sure, no problem. Consider it done."

The conversion process would involve installing new ATMs as well as replacing the software embedded in existing machines. The job had to be completed over a weekend—a December weekend, it turned out, when a major storm crippled traffic throughout the region. The company's trucks were stranded for hours on icy bridges, but on Monday morning the bank's cash machines were humming sweetly.

"Your organization, in particular Barbara David, performed in a most exemplary manner," wrote the bank's executive vice president to Barbara's top boss. "We . . . recognize efforts above and beyond and find it most comforting when our vendors respond to those levels. Please accept my congratulations for your team's efforts."

Of such stilted prose are resumés made. Within a few months, Barbara won an AT&T "quality performance" award for her work with the bank.

A year later, though, she was pulled off the account. Business is business.

Her relationship with this particular organization was always strained. By temperament, Barbara is someone who needs a sense of order, and the mid-level banker who was Barbara's contact on the account notes that this particular bank was often noncommittal. A different salesperson, he suggests, would have had an easier time accepting that fact.

The mid-level banker explains the modus operandi that prevailed when Barbara worked as an account executive (it has subsequently been reformed): Managers established a budget and got approval to purchase, say, forty ATMs—but it was not quite final approval. The bank and supplier had an understanding that the bank could always back out of the order at the last minute. Added to the mix was a difficult executive vice president, the man who was ultimately responsible for the firm's relationship with NCR and AT&T. His style, explains a banker who observed him in action for years was that he was the general, and everyone marched to his orders.

The bankers in this case had signed a major sales order, but still felt free to back out of a final portion of the deal, which represented about 30 percent of the total purchase. Several months later, they did. When the bank had pulled this stunt in the past, a purchase was only postponed; this time it was canceled. No one at NCR or AT&T had been blindsided like this before.

From the bankers' perspective, there was one problem. Since the firm was now buying fewer ATM machines than originally planned, it was entitled to a smaller price discount from AT&T. As a result, a special committee at the bank had to approve the purchase. In the midst of a major cost-cutting drive, this proved a public embarrassment for the ATM group.

Not long after, Barbara's boss was on the phone with the bank's executive vice president. The banker never asked that she be replaced as account executive, but his displeasure with Barbara was plain. Her old boss (who had recently retired) might have listened politely and hung up the phone, but Barbara's new supervisor took the opposite approach. "It's time for us to make a change," he told Barbara. "I'm taking you off the account."

Some of Barbara's colleagues could just as happily peddle car parts as cash machines. Selling is selling, many account executives would say with a shrug, but Barbara was never of that breed. She has a genuine interest and faith in the power of ATMs, part of her early fascination with interactive technology. Intrigued by their potential, in her final years at AT&T she pursued several opportunities to expand their domain beyond the basic cash machine. This enthusiasm, though, did not always stand her in good stead. Her bosses sometimes thought she should stick to the bread and butter of her business—selling ATMs to banks and thrifts.

After she lost her major bank account, Barbara stumbled upon an international deal that piqued her interest. Her office would often get phone calls from businessmen who would announce with great fanfare that they wanted to install five thousand ATMs—in China, say—and then were never heard from again. This particular project began with such a call. The notion was to sell thousands of ATMs to a network of small Russian and Georgian banks. From the beginning, Barbara sensed that this improbable story might actually end in a signed contract.

Her boss was dubious. The Russians said they were serious about buying the equipment, but who could be sure? They could simply decide not to buy anyone's ATMs, and that would be that. The winner got a contract, and everyone else walked away. And even if you got the contract, could you guarantee that the deal would be profitable rather than merely exotic?

But after a few months, Greg Vasil, Barbara's boss, decided that she should work full time on the Russian deal. A colleague took over her regular accounts. "We said to ourselves, we're going to win or we're going to lose, but let's give it our best shot," Greg recalls. "Barbara worked very hard on this project, sometimes too hard. There were times when I said, 'Back off. You're pushing people too hard.'"

And so, in 1995, as losses snowballed at NCR and layoffs became inevitable, Barbara assembled a team of AT&T executives who were frantically competing to win the bid to install ATMs in Moscow. She was convinced that the potential was enormous, and that her bosses had been playing it too safe.

Barbara turned out to be right about the Russians. The banking consortium did eventually sign a contract, but not with AT&T. "That was such an affirmation for me," Barbara says. "I wasn't crazy to pursue this. Someone actually got this contract."

In the final analysis, Barbara understood, her own imbroglios were playing out on a much larger canvas, whose colors were growing increasingly dark. By 1995, the former NCR (now part of AT&T's Global Information Solutions) was a deeply troubled business, with operating losses of $500 million for the first nine months of the year.

For the first couple of years after the acquisition of NCR, the ATM group remained autonomous, reporting to a single boss in Dayton, where NCR had its headquarters. By 1994, that structure had been shattered. Barbara's eight-person team, along with other ATM sales groups, reported to different bosses across the company as a horizontal organization replaced the established vertical structure. Where once Barbara and her colleagues could rely on information and support from executives focused exclusively on ATMs, now these bosses had other constituencies to serve. Not surprisingly, the company began to lose share in the ATM market.

By 1995, the turmoil of repeated restructuring in the sales division left Barbara and her coworkers reeling. No one knew when the organization charts would stop spinning. Barbara could make one prediction with certainty, though: another downsizing was coming, and this one would be deep.

The rumors began to build in July 1995; by Labor Day, everyone sensed that major layoffs would strike some time in September. No one suspected the bigger story—the trivestiture of AT&T that would accompany the announced downsizing. That secret was well kept.

Barbara was working at home on September 14th. She thought that her boss, Greg, would be meeting in New York City with his higher-ups. One of these days, she knew, he would be "coached"—that was the official phrase—on how to fire employees.

She called his office, and left a message on his voice mail. Greg called back an hour later. They began to talk about mundane office matters, and eventually moved on to the only real subject: the looming reorganization and what it would mean for their little sales team.

Greg knew what it would mean—people would lose their jobs. "I don't think we had exact numbers at this point, but we knew it would not be pretty," he says.

Barbara had worked with Greg for a year, and she had learned to hear the subtext in conversations with him. *Greg is a decent man,* Barbara said to herself, *and he's trying to send me a signal here. If my job were safe, he would probably let me know. But he's not.*

"I've been thinking about moving into consumer research," Barbara heard herself say.

"Maybe the time has come to make a clean break."

"Go for it," Greg told her. His voice was full of relief. "You'll do well in anything you choose to do. I'll do everything I can to help."

"Some people thought that what I did was a little rash," Barbara says. "But it was one of those moments when you know you're at an impasse and you feel the need to act."

A few weeks later, as Barbara recalls it, Greg told her that she had already been on the layoff list when they had this conversation. Greg does not remember if the names had already been identified at that point.

Officially, Barbara was downsized.

Out of habit as much as devotion, Barbara came into the office even after she was unemployed. She thought she would take some time to debrief the managers who had taken over her old accounts.

She did this for a few days before a young secretary approached her in the corridor. The woman worked for one of the bosses in the division. "I'm sorry," she said. "You're not supposed to be here." *The guy doesn't even have the guts to come out and tell me himself*, Barbara thought, but she said nothing. *Why am I here, anyway?* She packed up her bag and walked out the door.

She made her way to AT&T's resource center in Murray Hill, New Jersey, which became her new office. For Barbara the simple, physical fact of the place gave her a sense of control.

Most mornings she took the elevator down to the basement suite of offices, where she claimed her cubicle and computer. The data bank of job leads was actually quite good, she was pleased to discover. The traditional outplacement workshops proved helpful.

This was her first layoff, but she felt remarkably calm. "I knew I had to keep going," Barbara says. "I told myself that I must support myself, and my severance is not going to last long. So I need to work, but I also like to work. Being a businessperson is an important part of who I am."

She held on tight. Others in the resource center spoke bitterly about the downsizing and AT&T, but Barbara did not personalize the experience. She detached herself from the process, isolating her individual predicament from the abstract forces that drove the downsizing.

Her brother affectionately mocks Barbara's faith in management. Jim, a pharmacist, thinks of himself as a working man. Paid by the hour, his annual salary is not much less than his sister's compensation at AT&T, yet his world view is entirely different. "I'm a worker and she's an executive," he says with a chuckle. "I've had opportunities to go into management, but I never took them. I think if you become a manager, you have to be rotten. But even after the layoff, Barbara would argue that downsizing is sometimes necessary. I think you've got to let people work."

———————

"Talk to everyone you know," the outplacement counselors chanted. "One of them might tell you about your next job."

At her health club one afternoon, Barbara spotted her friend Howard, an investment adviser who had followed her Russian saga with interest. He had heard about a job opening at Diebold. It was a much smaller company than NCR, and it was starting up a new marketing department.

A vice president there was one of Howard's old friends. "Send him your resume," Howard told Barbara.

Federal Express delivered it two days later, and that same day Barbara received a call to come in for an interview. She had only been out of work for two weeks at this point, and the good news galvanized her faith and strength.

The meetings went well, though in the end the company hired someone else, a colleague from AT&T. With no recent marketing experience, Barbara knew that she was not the ideal candidate for this job. It reassured her, too, that the offer went to someone she respected.

"One question before you go," the Diebold executive said to Barbara as she called a cab for the airport. "Would you stay open to working in executive sales?"

Less than two weeks later, the same executive called Barbara back for a new round of interviews. A major corporate restructuring had claimed her old job at AT&T, and ironically it was a minor corporate restructuring that created her new job at Diebold.

At a meeting of senior management, the Diebold executives returned to a basic fact of their business: about 20 percent of the company's customers generated about 80 percent of its revenues. The executives reminded themselves that they had better take good care of these top accounts. To that end, they established a roster of fourteen national account teams.

In late 1995, when Barbara was looking for a job, Diebold had an opening for a team leader. Competing against her was an internal candidate, an account executive who was returning to the United States from a European posting. Barbara got the job.

Two moments in the application process were especially pleasing. During one interview, a senior executive told Barbara that he recalled reading her old master's thesis when it was published as an industry monograph in the late 1980s. He was impressed to learn that she was the author. At another point, the Diebold executives realized that their people had competed against Barbara to win the Russian contract, which was ultimately awarded to a joint venture of IBM and Diebold. They renewed their respect for a hardworking rival. Diebold, Barbara soon learned, was full of executives (including Bob Mahoney, the chairman) who had spent years working for NCR.

At Diebold, Barbara earns more money and assumes greater management responsibility than she did at AT&T. As a national team leader (the only woman at Diebold with that status), she manages two full-time and four part-time staffers.

When she joined the company, her bosses presented Barbara with a choice of two national accounts: a major bank, or an international financial services conglomerate. The banks were predictable and familiar. The conglomerate was complicated and sprawling, and for that reason it had been mostly ignored by ATM salespeople at both Diebold and NCR. But Barbara's instinct was that this company had tremendous untapped demand for Diebold products, and would be open to innovative applications of ATM technology. She decided to take the risk.

Barbara and her colleagues spent months courting their new client. Finally, just before the end of the year, the conglomerate placed a major purchase order and held out the promise of more business in the coming year.

Sales is a game of winners and losers. The order is signed, or it's not; the annual quota is filled, or it's not; the business goes to your company or its competitor. Barbara's first triumph, then, was especially sweet. The ATMs that Diebold will deliver to her new client will replace equipment that had been originally sold by NCR, Barbara's former employer and current rival.

———————

That was but one play in one inning, however, in a game that goes on forever. Though Diebold now feels to Barbara like an "oasis in corporate America," she knows that one day the sands may shift. Diebold's organizational structure is more collaborative and less competitive than NCR's. Still, Barbara says, "I don't assume that any corporate environment is static. Markets, industries and technologies all shift. You have to be prepared to pick yourself up and move with them. You have to depend, finally, on yourself." Business has become less forgiving. Flexibility, she has decided, is the only source of real strength.

Barbara came to that conclusion rationally, as the sober, sensible businesswoman she is. But it was also a visceral feeling, a natural product of her personal history. Whenever she has faced a loss in her life, she has said to herself—keep moving. And then she does.

5   LARRY NAGEL

Hunched over a computer terminal in a windowless office at Bell Labs—his thinning, sandy hair uncombed; a wrinkled shirt tail hanging out of his pants; papers spilling out of his pockets—Larry Nagel looked like an engineer. That is all he has ever wanted to be, ever since he was an only child building ham radio sets in Bakersfield, California. And that is what he was at UC Berkeley, where he earned a B.S. and Ph.D. in electrical engineering, and throughout his career at Bell Labs, a crown jewel of the old AT&T empire.

As a supervisor (the first level of management in the convoluted hierarchy of Bell Labs), Larry was a boss, too, but he never quite became a company man. The technical troops admired him—applauding his bluntness, tolerating his occasional tactlessness, and saluting him as one of their own. "Direct, straightforward, a breath of fresh air," says Sani Nassif, a technical staffer.

Larry is tall and has an open, kind face, with the touch of impishness that children find so appealing. He also has a middle-aged paunch and the requisite lines around his pale blue eyes, yet something survives of the tow-haired boy who loved to play outside in the California sun.

Throughout his career at AT&T, Larry would tell senior managers precisely what they did not want to hear. He has an engineer's faith in the power of reason: an electron is an electron is an electron, Larry says, and it's not negotiable. That faith was shared by Larry's old mentor, George Smith, one of the many Bell Labs legends—the man who invented the charge-coupled device (a critical component of the camcorder). In 1986 George decided to retire at the age of fifty-five taking off to sail around the world. Larry Nagel would not make such a graceful exit from the company that was his professional home for twenty years.

In November 1994, two weeks after his divorce became final, Larry learned that his job as a supervisor in the Computer-Aided Design Lab had been eliminated as part of a downsizing drive. Like most of his unlucky colleagues, Larry heard the news from his boss's boss. Lab director Bill Evans began his delivery with the classic refrain, "I'm sorry, I wish there were something we could do," followed by "You're getting the package." Larry was forty-eight when he heard this clumsy euphemism for "You're fired" for the first time.

A few minutes later, stunned and disoriented, Larry bumped into his coworkers Judy Schmidt and Scott McLaughlin. "This is what the package looks like," he said, attempting a laugh. Judy was shaken, her worst fears confirmed.

Everyone in the office knew that AT&T Microelectronics, the division with which the lab was linked, was vulnerable to layoffs because of its high R&D costs, and that supervisors might be sacrificed. Everyone also knew that a recent project of Larry's, a new kind of simulation software, had been a notorious and long-standing management mess, with three different bosses fighting for control. Nor were Larry's personal troubles any secret: since the start of the year, his wife had left him and filed for divorce; his mother had become ill; and Larry had made matters worse by drinking too much.

Most of all, there was a history of tension and conflict between Larry and his boss, Kishore Singhal. Kishore was a brilliant theorist, as aloof and professorial as Larry was blunt and earthbound. Though Bill Evans had signed off on the decision, Kishore almost certainly helped write the final coda to Larry's career at Bell Labs.

"Kishore wasn't gunning for Larry," says Sani Nassif. "But Larry had long been a thorn in his side. When the opportunity came to get rid of Larry, Kishore took it."

Says another of Larry's colleagues, "I do believe in my heart that Larry would still be at Bell Labs if he had worked for somebody else."

Four months after he was pushed out of AT&T, Larry landed a good job at Anadigics, a small New Jersey manufacturer of integrated circuits (which are crucial components in television set-top boxes and cellular phones). Compared to many of his downsized brethren, he was not unemployed long, and he now earns considerably more than he did at AT&T. He made his peace with the collapse of his twenty-year marriage and became absorbed in his work, his native self-confidence having been restored.

This hopeful synopsis earned Larry a sound bite on CNN when the cameras came calling during AT&T's 1996 downsizing to report on survivors of past layoffs. A less abridged version of his story is, of course, more complicated. Larry embarked upon a difficult mission, creating the second act of his life both personally and professionally. With an engineer's distaste for intangible psychological speculation, Larry sees his saga as a simple fight for survival: "I'm amazed that I did it. There were times when I wondered if I'd make it to the other side."

Before he turned thirty Larry had earned renown for his work as a brilliant UC Berkeley graduate student. In his Ph.D. dissertation, Larry created the Spice software program; the name is an acronym for Simulation Program with Integrated Circuit Emphasis. Its 22,000 lines of code predict the electrical performance of circuits before the chips are built, thereby saving designers considerable time and expense. Spice quickly became an industry standard and its derivatives are widely used to this day, a remarkable achievement in the ever-changing software business. (One of the early users of Spice, as it happens, was a Bell Labs engineer named Bill Evans, who would later fire its author.)

Larry's Berkeley days were cheerful and uncomplicated. He arrived in the fall of 1964, just in time for the Free Speech Movement. Larry considered himself a good liberal, but he was always more interested in algorithms than demonstrations.

On the evening of his nineteenth birthday, in the fall of his sopho-more year, Larry went to a college mixer at nearby Mills College and met Harriet Silverblatt, a shy eighteen-year-old who had grown up in an affluent Jewish family in St. Louis. She and Larry were soon insepa-rable and in June 1968, at the end of Larry's senior year, they married.

By this time, Larry had found his life's work, which was really a re-turn to his childhood love for electronics. The passion has clearly sus-tained him into middle age. "What I love about electronics," he says with unaffected enthusiasm, "is that you conceive of something, and then you get to see it work. There is a tangible manifestation of your idea, and you can hold it in your hands."

This is an engineer, his daughter Laura would later joke, with ab-solutely no affinity for chaos theory. "He likes things to be rational," she says. "He likes to add things up and see what you get."

The ham radios of eighth grade made way at Berkeley to the mas-sive mainframes of the mid-1960s. "I really fell for computers," Larry says, "beginning with an IBM 7094—it filled up several rooms—on which I learned how to program in FORTRAN, one of the original computer programming languages."

In a research seminar in his senior year, he met Professor Don Ped-erson. Pederson introduced Larry to the thrill of making integrated cir-cuits ("those beautiful gleaming wafers," Larry calls them). In a course with another Berkeley professor, Ron Rohrer, Larry helped lead a class project to write a circuit simulation program. This project was the ker-nel of what would become the Spice software.

This original program (called Cancer) was technically promising despite its name, but the two professors vehemently disagreed about its future. An old-fashioned academic, Pederson thought the software should be in the public domain, while Rohrer was eager to make some money from it. Since Pederson, the senior member of the faculty, wouldn't budge, Rohrer left Berkeley to work in the private sector.

Pederson encouraged Larry to keep working on the software proj-ect. "We're really on a roll here," he told Larry one summer afternoon after Larry's first year of graduate school. "Why don't you explore all the algorithms, test them out, and make it your Ph.D. dissertation?"

"Sounds great," Larry said, and immediately took off to tell his wife.

They were the traditional graduate school couple, the intense student and the devoted spouse, both of them content with the stereotype. Harriet worked as a nursery school teacher until their first daughter, Laura, was born in 1971. Another daughter, Becky, was born three years later.

As a Ph.D. candidate working on his circuit simulator (he had by this time changed the name to Spice) Larry's workday began at noon and ended at about 1:00 am. Larry would shuttle between a small office and the math building, where he used the university's powerful new computer. By now, Berkeley had a CDC 6400. On this mainframe Larry ran his "cards," the envelope-sized IBM punch cards that constituted a computer program.

After he ate dinner with his wife and played with his baby, Larry would walk downstairs to his basement study: "a dank, dingy, windowless little place," Larry recalls, right next to the laundry room. It was here that he did his best work.

"Larry was obsessed with quality and detail," Ron Rohrer says of his former student. Like many engineers, he could sometimes be obsessive about things that did not merit any attention at all. When Larry was harnessed to a worthy cause, his focus could be extremely productive. "Pointed in the right direction, Larry can be tenacious," says Dick Dowell, a fellow engineer who was a few years ahead of Larry at Berkeley and was to become a lifelong friend.

Creating Spice was unquestionably Larry's finest hour. Within just a few years of its introduction, it redefined how circuit engineers around the world go about their work. Virtually everyone working in integrated circuits today knows the name Spice—and many of them also know, from their college and graduate school textbooks, that the father of Spice is a fellow named Larry Nagel.

"Not all of us get our fifteen minutes of fame," Larry says. "Spice was mine." It was also his ticket to Bell Labs.

Larry would produce nothing as original during his career at AT&T. Yet fame at a tender age instilled in Larry a great reserve of self-confidence, which would help pull him through when he was cut loose and alone.

If engineers are natural loners who find what companionship they need in the company of their colleagues, Larry's childhood seems to have prepared him well for his future. Solitude was a familiar state; his friends were fellow techies.

He grew up in the middle-class town of Bakersfield, in the heart of the Central Valley, about a hundred miles north of Los Angeles. In the 1950s and early 1960s, most of Bakersfield's 100,000 residents were attached to one of the two pillars of the local economy—cotton and oil. Larry's father worked for the county public health department, inching his way up from sanitation inspector to mid-level civil servant. His mother stayed home until Larry was in high school, when she went back to work as a chemist.

"My parents were very aloof," Larry says, characteristically unable to elaborate beyond that simple statement. Devoted to each other, Larry's mother and father kept their distance from their only child. Neither demanding nor giving, they were essentially uninvolved.

"My grandparents were not emotional people," says Laura, now twenty-five, "and I imagine my father was never completely sure how they felt about him." On one of the few occasions that Larry took his children back to California, Laura recalls a single tableau: The extended family would gather in the modern living room, watching the sun stream through skylights built into a cathedral ceiling. Long stretches of silence were punctuated by casual commentaries on innocuous subjects: the neighbors, local politics, the weather. "It was the kind of chat you'd expect from a stranger sitting next to you on a park bench," Larry says.

Left to his own devices as a child, Larry found his diversions and amusements in predictable places. The family had a dog, a dachshund named Cocoa, whom Larry adored. Once he received a crystal radio for his tenth birthday, Larry's interest in how things work became evident. His greatest delight came in tinkering, taking something apart and putting it back together for no other reason than to see how it worked.

During a typical evening, Larry would reassemble the radio and stay up late listening to the Bakersfield Bears, the local minor league ballclub. Soon he found the great distraction of his youth, ham radio. More than thirty years later, Larry can reel off his ham call number as well as the numbers of his two pals: "Mike Gibson was WA6MWA, Steve Hopkins was WA6MZQ, and I was WA6MYG."

"Heaven was five dollars and an afternoon to spend plowing through a pile of junk transmitters and receivers at an Army surplus store," he says.

Money was tight, though. Both his parents had been frightened by the Depression, and while his father made a solid wage, the occasional restaurant dinner or movie was almost always dismissed as an unjustifiable extravagance. There were no trips to the zoo, and it still bothers Larry that the family never made it to Disneyland. As a father, he worked hard to give his own children what he feels he missed. "I was probably a pain in the neck," he says, "hanging around too much, but I was definitely involved."

Yet his father's frugality did not inspire Larry to try to make a fortune. If Larry had left Berkeley in the wake of Spice and made his way to the venture capitalists of Silicon Valley instead of the rumpled academics of Bell Labs, he might have built a software company and eventually sold it for millions. Years later friends would tease him about his road not taken, but the ribbing was good-natured: Larry knew that he was never meant to be a daring entrepreneur. "I was looking for a steady paycheck, like everyone else," he says.

Larry's Ph.D. dissertation was not yet finished when Don Scharfetter recruited him to Bell Labs. The bosses wanted to get Larry on the payroll by the end of 1974; the following year, a hiring freeze would be in effect.

Larry's first major assignment was adapting the Spice software to meet the particular demands of AT&T's business. Other companies would be doing much the same thing, since the program was in the public domain, but AT&T had a great asset in having the author on staff.

By December 1976 Larry had finished writing most of the code that would comprise the new software (which had been dubbed "Advice"), but that was only the beginning. Adopting such a complicated program, AT&T's users would need a great deal of support before they could comfortably manage it on their own. Moreover, as problems arose, the software would have to be modified. Larry spent the better part of the next eight years working on Advice. "It was a real feather in his cap and a major contribution to AT&T," says Colin McAndrew, Larry's colleague in his final years with the company.

This triumph was never repeated. Colin has great respect for Larry's talent and achievement, but he believes that after Advice, "Larry never found anything to really sink his teeth into. He wasn't challenged as he should have been. That is a failing of senior management, but it can also be seen as Larry's personal failure."

───────────

Bell Labs could be a hive of egos as well as imagination. Larry's career, like many, was touched by a noisy clash of personalities. A talented and blunt Berkeley Ph.D., Larry squared off against Kishore Singhal, a talented, remote, Indian-born scientist.

The world of circuit engineering is a small one, and so Kishore and Larry had known each other's work for years before they first met. Kishore was a highly respected professor at the University of Waterloo in Canada in 1982 when he contemplated moving to the United States. In the spring of that year he called Larry Nagel, whom he knew by reputation. "I'm looking for a summer position," Kishore said on the phone. "Might there be an opportunity to work at Bell Labs?"

"I'll see what I can do," Larry replied. He had read many of Kishore's papers, which he thought were brilliant, and he was honored by the request.

Later that day, Larry went in to speak with Hermann Gummel, his department head at Bell Labs. Kishore soon signed on for a year's sabbatical and joined Gummel's department; Larry served as his supervisor.

Kishore joined Bell Labs full time and became a manager, but the former academic never modulated his style. "He was the professor and you were his graduate student," says Sani Nassif. To many of his subordinates, the style could grate. Sani was especially annoyed by one of Kishore's managerial quirks: "If he needed to speak to you, he'd come and stand in front of your office and wave a little finger at you" like a wayward third grader.

Larry, however, refused to play along. When a contest of egos started between Larry and Kishore, none of their colleagues was surprised. "Both men have strong personalities, they're both very well-known in their fields. A clash was not unexpected," says Prasad Subramaniam, who worked with both men as a product manager.

The tension between Larry and Kishore began to build when Larry joined Bill Evans's lab in 1991, and it escalated dramatically after January 1993. The catalyst was actually a piece of good news for the lab: AT&T Microelectronics, the business unit of AT&T that funded the lab's research, was pleased with the group's progress on its Celerity software project. This was a piece of simulation software being designed to replace Advice, the Spice derivative that Larry had worked on for so long.

Larry had been involved in Celerity from its inception in 1991, but he always harbored mixed feelings about its fate. He had a parental pride in Advice, which was still widely used within AT&T. Celerity's success would mark the end of its reign. "Sometimes he felt that Celerity's success would be like killing his child," says John Tauke, a product manager in the lab and one of Larry's friends. At the same time, even Larry acknowledged that Advice, however functional, was looking a little long in the tooth.

A year of messy and sometimes bitter conflicts ensued from a classic case of bad management. Peter Lloyd, the department head, had named three supervisors to the Celerity project: Larry, Kishore, and Sally Liu, who had been supervising the development of Advice in recent years. Sally was the first UC Berkeley graduate recruited by Larry when he returned to his alma mater on behalf of AT&T; in later years, though, Larry could be one of her fiercest critics. Some of his colleagues, especially Kishore, thought that Larry was much harsher than he needed to be.

Why set up such an unwieldy management structure? Perhaps Lloyd thought that three different perspectives and areas of expertise would produce some useful synergies. What transpired, instead, was mostly chaos. At one point, Sani Nassif, who was acting as the lead technical person on the project, went into Lloyd's office to try to force a change. "Everyone's managing everything," he pleaded with Lloyd. But nothing was done.

Finally, in the spring of 1994, Sani felt so besieged by the problems and politics that he dropped out of the Celerity team. Since Sani reported to Larry and was also a friend, his presence on the team had helped Larry's standing. When he left, Larry's fading star dimmed even more.

"If I had been smart," Larry later remarked, "when the Celerity project got into trouble, I would have cut my losses and looked for another job within AT&T."

His position became precarious around April of 1994, when Peter Lloyd took a leave from AT&T to work for Sematech, the prestigious research facility funded by the top American technology companies. Kishore was named as Lloyd's temporary successor, becoming acting head of the department—and, alarmingly, Larry's immediate boss. Larry did not expect to get the post, but it still felt like a slap in the face to be bested by his rival. Kishore pulled Larry off the Celerity team; from now on, Sally would be running the show.

How could Larry possibly step aside? Despite the problems and turmoil, circuit simulation was his life's work. The code was in his blood.

"Larry was attached to the project, emotionally and intellectually," says Judy. "When he was taken off the team, it was a blow to his ego, and he had a hard time letting go." Convinced Sally was not up to the job, Larry would occasionally comment on changes or suggest revisions. This caused even more friction with Kishore, who admired Sally's work.

Stripped of his role on Celerity, Larry found himself relatively underoccupied at precisely the moment that Bell Labs and AT&T Microelectronics executives were facing the latest corporate directive to cut costs. Layoffs were a real threat.

In the way that downward spirals can take on the force of gravity, Larry's problems at the lab exacerbated the tensions in his marriage. By the end of 1994, he would lose both his marriage and his job.

Larry has a tremendous capacity to deny what he does not want to see, and he spent most of 1994 oblivious to the threats that he faced. The year began with a difficult trip to California. In the middle of January, Larry's seventy-six-year-old mother entered the hospital for surgery to treat hydrocephalus. Larry spent two weeks visiting her and doing what he could to comfort his seventy-four-year-old father, whose own health was failing. These were never simple reunions, and this visit was wrenching, as Larry knew it would be.

About a month after Larry returned home to New Jersey, Harriet delivered a speech that was all the more impassioned for being long suppressed.

It's over, she told her husband. Our marriage is dead. A reconciliation is impossible.

The couple had been emotionally estranged for years and they had discussed the possibility of a divorce. For the first time, though, Larry heard a note of finality in his wife's voice.

Larry believes that his marriage became hopeless when Harriet befriended a colleague at Rutgers, where she worked as nursery school director. The two married a few months after her divorce from Larry became final. "My current husband was not the reason we divorced," Harriet says. "We went to three different marriage counselors over ten years. There were longstanding problems."

When Larry looks back a few years later, his direct, plainspoken manner understates the depth of his hurt. "No one likes to get pitched out in the street for another," he says now with a strained smile. At the time, though, his wife's rejection enraged him.

Larry and Harriet continued to live together for another two months. Larry held onto the fantasy of a second chance, but the sunny rooms of their house were filled with angry recriminations and malevolent glares. Fortunately, their daughter Becky's upstairs corner bedroom was now empty—they had driven her up to Oberlin that fall—so she could no longer hear the spasms of her parents' dying marriage.

It was a snowy Saturday afternoon in the middle of March when the final explosion came. "I was watching a stock car race, and I'd been drinking, when I went outside to get the mail," Larry recalls. A letter from his wife's lawyer had arrived. A few hours later, when Harriet returned home, Larry handed the letter to her.

"I thought we agreed you wouldn't hire this lawyer!" Larry shouted at her. "He's too expensive!"

"I'll hire whoever I want!" came Harriet's unyielding reply.

In a drunken rage, Larry shoved his wife, who would later file a restraining order against him. She picked up the phone and dialed 911, but Larry grabbed the receiver and slammed it down.

Harriet raced to her car and took off.

"Then I did the stupidest thing in the world," Larry says. He got into his car and followed his wife to her friend's house, where he knew she would be. A local policeman had already arrived. Larry was arrested for drunk driving, and his license was suspended for six months.

Looking at the police report two years later, Larry remembers the immeasurable despair he felt that day. "The defendant starts to cry," the policeman wrote. "He states that he has nothing to live for. He states that when he gets home he will be putting a gun to his head. He also states that his kids will be better off without him."

The shame of the arrest would linger for months, but the crisis brought a certain relief to Larry: "I could see for the first time that my marriage was really over."

There was one immediate problem. Without a license, Larry couldn't drive from New Jersey to the headquarters of AT&T Microelectronics in Allentown, Pennsylvania, where he had been working with his Bell Labs department colleagues since 1991. Eight of his AT&T friends joined Larry on a misty day in late March—Harriet's birthday, as it turned out—to help him pack for the move to Allentown. "I had reached the lowest point of my life," Larry says, "and I was very touched that my friends came through for me."

Larry had the doggedness of the devoted engineer: you just keep going until the equation is solved. Even if he was anxious or unhappy, he could still throw himself into his work.

When he was assigned to work as a member of a small, ISO quality control team, Larry took it on with enthusiasm. Though it was perceived by many as a thankless task, Larry saw it as a useful distraction from his troubles, and a worthwhile job in its own right.

ISO was a project delivered from the higher echelons of AT&T Microelectronics. ISO, which stands for International Standards Organization, is a quality assurance certificate. Bill Evans's lab, along with others, would have to quickly correct any of its quality problems.

Judy worked closely with Larry on ISO. When Larry's sad year came to an end, she was convinced of one thing: "This assignment was the straw that broke the camel's back."

What came with the turf—and this is part of what appealed to Larry about the job—was the absolute necessity of alienating senior management. The ISO team members were the equivalent of school hall monitors, but instead of tattling on misbehaving students, they were reporting their own teachers. And Larry never could hold his tongue.

His aversion to office politesse and bureaucratic maneuvers was invariably self-defeating. Like many universities, Bell Labs was swarming with independent, creative minds who somehow conspired to produce an institution that could be rigidly hierarchical and stultifyingly petty. Yet Larry's anti-establishment streak was also a hallmark of the pure techie: something either works or it doesn't; and if it doesn't work, it should be fixed.

Larry's candor was especially dangerous on the ISO project. "Unless they are delicately handled, quality efforts alienate people," Judy explains. "You're frequently telling people things they don't want to hear. You can't necessarily come at people straight, and Larry comes at people very straight."

Each member of the ISO team was responsible for determining the problems and failings of his or her own department, the procedures that were vulnerable to criticism from an ISO inspector. Larry's job, and that of his counterparts, was to report to director Bill Evans on the failings of their bosses. It seems almost comic that Larry was assigned to document the failings of Kishore, his longtime nemesis, but that was the untenable position in which he was placed.

Typically, he was blind to the real danger he faced.

After Larry and his colleagues had made a preliminary report to Bill Evans, the lab director convened a meeting. The ISO project was one item on the agenda. "What is wrong with your department? What are you doing to fix it?" Bill asked Kishore directly during the meeting. He was calm—Bill Evans was never one to lose his temper—but no one could miss the steely edge in his voice.

At another meeting, Bill Evans publicly suggested to Kishore that annual performance reviews would be affected by poor ISO ratings. "Larry's in big trouble now," one of his colleagues remarked when news of the meeting got out.

At another juncture in the history of AT&T, Larry might have eluded his enemies. But it was 1994, and his division, like others in AT&T that year, was being downsized. A 10 percent cut in payroll costs would be imposed across the board. (As with most AT&T layoffs, the actual cuts achieved would be far less.)

"Maybe the lesson is, if you're not getting along with your boss, you'd better look for another job." Looking back, Larry recalls one conversation with Kishore that was perhaps meant as a warning, though Larry did not hear that message at the time.

"I can't have a supervisor working on just these two projects," Kishore told Larry some time in September or October of 1994, referring to Larry's work on ISO and his other assignment, Interconnect. (This was an effort to study how electrons move through the several layers of metal that link the millions of transistors built into an integrated circuit.)

Larry agreed that he was underoccupied. "What should we do to fix this?" he asked.

"Let's think about it," Kishore replied. The two men exchanged a few awkward pleasantries at that point, and the subject was never again addressed.

"Maybe he was trying to plant the idea that I might be vulnerable in a future downsizing," Larry would later observe. "But no one told me that. I knew I was in a mess. But all my evaluations had been good. I had absolutely no inkling that my career was in jeopardy."

After a decade of downsizing at AT&T, layoffs developed a predictable rhythm. Typically, the overture lasts a few weeks, as rumors begin to build. Then reality strikes.

How many millions of American workers first learn about their company layoffs in a conference room or auditorium? A sudden summons to these cheerless arenas almost always brings bad news.

After the morning e-mail directed them to a conference room, Larry and a few hundred managers at Bell Labs and AT&T Microelectronics gathered to hear what few facts would be divulged. The rumors were true (they almost always are)—layoffs were coming. The downsizing would unfold in the usual AT&T fashion: People would be placed in "universes" and rated according to various categories. Neither the universes nor the categories were precisely defined.

The news was delivered as a joint pronouncement by Bill Evans and a representative from human resources. There is always a representative from human resources at these affairs, and no one ever remembers his name.

There would be "packages." (Some of the newer employees may have wondered why their higher-ups couldn't speak in English, but AT&T had its own rituals, and after one downsizing everyone learned what the words really meant.)

People could volunteer to quit; in the vernacular, they'd "take" the package. Their unlucky brethren would be "given" the package, or learn that they had been "considered" for the package and ultimately "accepted"—which meant that they had 60 days to find another job within the company. In a dissonant echo of the college-admissions game, workers learned their status when they saw the size of their envelope: A thin envelope meant that you kept your job. A thick envelope was the "package" itself, full of pension equations and health benefit calculations. In short, a thick envelope was bad news.

The staff was told to circle November 15th on their calendars. That surprised no one; layoffs traditionally began just before the start of the Christmas season.

On the morning of Thursday, November 15th (predictably dubbed Black Thursday), Larry received the envelopes for his own staff. He was relieved to see they were all thin. After an hour or two, though, he began to worry: why hadn't Kishore distributed the envelopes to the supervisors in his group?

Larry walked to his boss's office. "Kishore, am I getting the package?" he asked as he stood in the doorway. Kishore seemed uneasy.

"I don't know," Kishore replied, "we have to talk to Bill Evans."

"Let's go, then," Larry said.

"I have to see if he's available. Why don't you go back to your office and wait?"

Larry sat at his desk for about ten minutes before the phone rang. It was Bill. "Why don't you come by?" he asked.

Bill was standing and Kishore was sitting when Larry walked in. His eyes immediately focused on the answer to his question: a thick envelope lying dead center on an otherwise empty table.

"Larry, you got the package," Bill said. Larry looked straight at Kishore, who turned away.

"This is terrible," Bill continued, "but there's nothing we can do about it." *You did this to me*, Larry thought to himself; *there is everything you can do about it*. Then his head began to spin. *It's a joke*.

For a few seconds he actually believed they were kidding; it couldn't be real. Larry could feel the anger building. "My ears got warm, and I could feel my skin getting flushed. My heart was racing, and my muscles tensed." He summoned all his strength to contain his rage, and he kept silent.

A few days later, Larry spoke to Bill alone. "He wanted me to believe that this was none of his doing. I've had to fire people a few times, and I hate it. But if I do it, I don't pretend it's something over which I have no control. . . . Bill couldn't even take responsibility for what he'd done."

There was a brief mention of the cause of Larry's misfortune: poor teamwork. That was the performance category, it seemed, in which he scored a failing grade. Larry told Bill what a laugh this was—the ISO team was the essence of effective teamwork.

"I helped save your bacon on that team," Larry told him.

But Bill just shrugged and looked away. "I wish there were something I could do."

One week after Larry picked up his thick envelope, Kishore and another department supervisor took the Interconnect team out to lunch—to honor the group for its fine teamwork. As a member of the team, Larry came along. No one mentioned the obvious irony.

Like so many forty-eight-year-olds who are downsized in American corporations, Larry signed a waiver that entitled him to a 20 percent bonus on his severance package if he promised not to sue AT&T. Privately, though, he wondered at the company's orchestration of his dismissal. There were four supervisors in his department, Larry knew. He thought the lineup was clear: Colin was the supervisor in charge of modeling; Peter Zeitzoff was the supervisor in charge of computer-aided design technology; and he and Sally were the supervisors responsible for circuit simulation.

If people were to be grouped in universes of similar skills—as the human resources rhetoric had it—shouldn't he and Sally be paired off? They essentially had the same job. But in the fine print of his package, AT&T explained, Larry and Peter Zeitzoff had become a pair. "We were both middle-aged men. They could have paired me with Sally, but then maybe they'd worry about a discrimination lawsuit."

The company's categories were based on geography, a company spokesman explains. Sally Liu worked in New Jersey, so she was in one universe; because Larry and Peter Zeitzoff were based in Pennsylvania, they lived in a different universe.

Among Larry's former colleagues, it was months after the downsizing before a black mood lifted. "I was really in shock," says Sani. So too was Prasad Subramaniam, who would be promoted in 1996 to become the head of Larry's old department. "It was a surprise to me and to a lot of people that someone of Larry's stature would be laid off. I personally talked to all the managers I could to try to dissuade them from doing this."

"We knew that in other labs, the decision [was] made to eliminate the poorest performers," says another one of his colleagues. "But this group didn't seem to work that way. During the three downsizings I've been through, there are people who are notoriously poor performers, and everyone knows it, and they stay. That's what was one of the hardest things about Larry's leaving. Here's a guy who is still a name in his field—okay, maybe he was having an off year in 1994, but he had done good work until that point—and he's leaving, while we see people who do nothing, and they stay."

"Here was a man with such an illustrious career, to be so cavalierly removed," adds Sani. Though he himself was regarded as a top performer in the lab, Sani began to think about his own future at AT&T, where he had worked for eight years after receiving his Ph.D. in electrical engineering from Carnegie Mellon. "I better watch out," Sani told his wife a few days after Larry was fired. "Who knows who will be next?" About a year later, Sani took a job at IBM.

For the better part of a decade, Bell Labs had been losing some of its most talented scientists. When AT&T was still a regulated monopoly, the budget of the labs had been extraordinarily generous—outside of academia, there was no more comfortable place to do scientific research. The more recent exodus reflects the unavoidable reality that research has been increasingly affected by the pressures of the commercial market. Larry's departure, then, was seen in this larger context: You sit back and allow all these big names to quit, and now you're pushing another one out the door?

For weeks, Larry still could not quite believe that his career at Bell Labs was coming to an end. "Getting fired completely blindsided me," he says. At a reception hall at the Allentown Hilton, where he joined about a hundred of his colleagues for a day of outplacement counseling, the word *denial* bounced off the parquet floors and chandeliers.

As a young man, Larry imagined that he would stay married until he died; he expected to work for Bell Labs until he retired. After all, his father had worked for the state of California for twenty-eight years, until he retired at age 55; his parents had stayed together through 51 years of marriage. Larry's youthful expectations were typical of his generation—but now they seemed a silent and painful rebuke.

"He seemed a shell of a person," says Sani. "You'd talk to him, and he seemed in a different world." Larry's daughter Laura could hear the anxiety in his voice, even as her father tried to keep up the facade of the capable, protective parent. "He wouldn't talk about it directly, but I knew he was depressed," says Laura. It was harder to get him off the phone, she recalls with amused affection. They didn't discuss the layoff or Larry's job prospects, but spent a lot of time talking about music.

At the eleventh hour, AT&T made Larry a final offer: he could accept a demotion to work in another department of Bell Labs. By this time, even though Larry had no other job offers, he knew he had to leave.

Slowly, almost imperceptibly, he regained his equilibrium. Going off on job interviews made a tremendous difference, his daughter and his friends could see. "He had asked himself, 'Am I of use to anyone? Will anyone find me useful again?'" Laura says. "Larry is fundamentally a confident person," adds Sani, "and this was a real crisis of confidence."

By the end of January, Larry received a job offer from Crystal Semiconductor in Austin, Texas, and another from Anadigics. The salaries and responsibilities were similar, but Anadigics was a fast-growing firm that actually manufactured circuits. In the lingo, Anadigics had a fabrication line, Larry explains, while Crystal was "fab-less." To the boy who liked to reassemble ham radios, the "fab line" had a real appeal. At Anadigics, Larry supervises circuit designers, and he can see the tangible results of their labor.

Just before he arrived at Anadigics, the company issued a press release, boasting of its good fortune in hiring the father of Spice. Less than a year later, Larry was promoted.

After he left AT&T, Larry was alternately amused and vindicated by some of the news that filtered back from his old department.

First came word that Larry's old lab director, Bill Evans, was himself under pressure; his lab—and, with it, his own status and authority—appeared vulnerable. Eventually, though, senior management decided to move the lab out of the Microelectronics group and back to Bell Labs, where its research would have a better chance to flourish. Evans's position was further bolstered when his lab secured some funding from Sematech, the prestigious industry consortium, to help defray expenses. Such is the art of corporate survival.

Larry could not help but be pleased to hear that Kishore's temporary assignment to become acting department head—the move that preceded Larry's dismissal—did not become permanent. Within several months of Larry's departure, two supervisors (Colin McAndrew and Sani Nassif) had bailed out of Kishore's department. By 1996, Sally Liu was gone as well. No one blamed Kishore, but he had to acknowledge that his empire was shrinking. In the end, Prasad Subramaniam, the young man who was so impressed to meet the father of Spice when he first came to interview at Bell Labs, took over the department. Kishore moved into another part of the company.

The Celerity project on which Larry, Kishore, and Sally had battled so long was deemed a success. By the spring of 1997, about 90 percent of the potential users inside the company had converted to the new software, while the remainder had stuck with Larry's old warhorse, Advice. Larry was amused to hear that while he was still working at AT&T, product manager John Tauke had ordered up marketing brochures touting the fact that Celerity was in part the handiwork of Larry Nagel, the father of Spice. The brochures were eventually thrown in the trash.

Not long after the 1994 downsizing that swept up Larry Nagel, the Microelectronics group found itself understaffed and launched a hiring spree, though it did not extend to Larry's old lab. "We fire people and within months, we're hiring at a frenetic pace," says Tauke. "It just seems so unnecessary." The hiring binge continued throughout 1995, even as the rest of the company was hit with layoffs. The silicon business grew tremendously during the year, and the division's integrated circuits—used in cellular phones, laser printers, and computer peripherals—were in widespread demand. Tauke himself spent more and more time interviewing potential recruits. Who is the company looking for? "People like Larry," he says with a chuckle. "People with the same sort of skills. He'd be extremely marketable here."

That did not surprise Larry, since he had witnessed the same pattern through past waves of downsizing. The random force of corporate bureaucracies can never be underestimated; Larry had learned that much during his twenty years at AT&T.

Even for an engineer, Larry is remarkably free of any impulse toward introspection. Still, when he looks back on what was clearly the most difficult year of his life, he recognizes that it forced him to redefine his personal identity in ways that were both painful and positive.

Larry now accepts the fact that his marriage could not be salvaged. He also recognizes that he had grown stale clinging to the status and ultimately false security of Bell Labs. "If I had not been given a kick, I probably would have hung around another seven years until retirement," he says. "And that would have been a waste."

He feels driven now to redeem himself, "to prove that the guys who got rid of me made a mistake." But he has found himself in his work in ways that are anything but petty. Larry feels once again the simple joy of watching gleaming wafers roll off an assembly line. Starting over at age fifty, Larry has reclaimed the spirit of the young engineer who wrote thousands of lines of software in a dank Berkeley basement.

A RETURN TO THE FOLD

Maggie Starley, a displaced telephone operator, and Kyle Stevens, a mid-level business strategist, returned to outposts of the old AT&T empire as company rebels. Maggie's defiance dates back to her days as a nineteen-year-old union steward. Kyle's came after years of corporate devotion and stagnation, when he realized that he was becoming a Fortune 500 version of his father, a thirty-year navy man. Now they both subscribe to a bald individualism, which Kyle defines in a single question: "What's in it for me?"

6   MAGGIE STARLEY

In the winter of 1996, Maggie's Pet Sitting was a failing business—a fact that came as no surprise to Maggie Starley, the feisty, curly-haired woman who was its sole proprietor (and lone pet sitter). This was Binghamton, New York, a city still reeling from the massive IBM layoffs three years before. Who had the money to pay someone to baby-sit their golden retrievers?

At the age of forty-two, Maggie had worked as a telephone operator at AT&T for twenty-three years when the company shut down its Binghamton office in 1994. That decision was part of a major downsizing that eliminated about 5,500 operator jobs in thirty-seven offices that year. Since the layoff, Maggie had been scuffling along, looking for paralegal jobs (she had gotten her degree while working at AT&T), settling for secretarial stints arranged through a temporary employment agency. These assignments rarely paid much more than minimum wage, a sharp retreat from Maggie's old AT&T salary of $562 a week.

She hoped that the pet-sitting scheme would pay at least a few household expenses. There were the $813-a-month mortgage payments on the small house that she and her boyfriend, John, another downsized AT&T operator, had bought in 1992. They'd take a big loss if they were forced to sell. She couldn't even begin to think about buying a new car, but her ten-year-old Toyota truck had a hundred thousand miles on it and probably wouldn't survive another winter.

When the phone rang one evening in January 1996, it was one of

Maggie's old managers on the other end. Had she heard? AT&T was hiring in Syracuse—now.

The company was expanding its customer service operations, the manager continued. You're either answering questions on the phone or punching in names and numbers at a computer terminal. She didn't know many more details, but she was sure that the job paid well.

There was a qualifying test, but a number of former operators had passed it. Maggie was bright, the manager said; she'd be fine.

Indeed she was. A few weeks later, Maggie was hired as a "customer sales and support representative" (CSSS, for short), handling the problems of the company's large corporate customers. On May 13, 1996, almost two years after she lost her job as an operator, she rejoined AT&T. It was an odd homecoming.

Gregarious and defiantly cheerful, Maggie is a tireless talker, especially if the subject is politics or her two boisterous dogs, both Labrador–German shepherd crosses. Like the jolly partygoer who gets everyone out on the dance floor, she draws people to her. "I do get down sometimes, but I don't let myself stay down for any length of time," Maggie says. "Life's too damn short."

A one-time union activist—she was elected a steward of the Communications Workers of America (CWA) when she was just nineteen years old—Maggie believes that labor and management are inevitably divided by different class interests. Unlike many of her colleagues, she never had any illusions that AT&T was anyone's benevolent family. When she was downsized in 1994, she understood that technology had killed her job, as it had killed tens of thousands of operator jobs since the 1950s.

"This is a company that fundamentally doesn't give a damn about its employees," Maggie said a few weeks before her first day's orientation as a returning employee at AT&T. "They use you and dispose of you. That makes them no different than most other American companies, I suppose. You can't hate them for that. But I have very mixed emotions about going back to AT&T."

She returned for the same reason that she first joined the company as a seventeen-year-old high school graduate: it's a good job that pays well. Without her AT&T salary, Maggie could keep just a few steps ahead of the working poor. Maggie's inability to afford medical insurance after she left the AT&T payroll was a brusque reminder of that fact.

"I cannot get a better-paying job," she says, "certainly not in upstate New York, and not many other places either." Most critically, the contract between AT&T and the CWA union, which represents occupational workers, ensured that she regained her seniority when she returned to the company. If Maggie can keep working there for another six years, she will reach a critical number—unlike its managers, AT&T's occupational workers can claim a full pension at any age, as long as they have thirty years of service.

"I'm trying to get in as many years as I can," Maggie says. "I also understand that if tomorrow AT&T changes its business plans, I'm a flea they'll shake off. Everyone is expendable, and every layoff starts with the peons."

On a cool spring day, as the sun slips in and out of the clouds, Maggie sits on the deck of her house. Out front is a well-tended garden, full of roses, pansies, and petunias. Inside, the house is a cozy mess of chairs and sofas, worn carpeting, and stacks of magazines. As she takes a guilty drag on a cigarette (she's down to two packs a day—it used to be three), Maggie thinks about the course of her life in this small city. Except for a brief marriage that took her to Florida for a few months, she has lived in the Binghamton area since she was born.

The youngest of six children, Maggie is her mother's daughter. "Esther was a survivor," Maggie says of her mother, a fast-talking lady with fiery blue eyes who died in 1995 at the age of seventy-three. "She was honest, and she gave me a sense of right and wrong. I like to think I acquired her independence."

For thirty-five years, Esther worked for the GAF company, standing on a cement floor, picking up boxes of film that weighed up to fifty pounds, and loading them onto planks of wood. "It was hard work,"

Maggie says. Her father worked as a bread delivery man and as a laborer in a post-office warehouse, but he didn't tend to hold a steady job. "What can I say?" Maggie asks. "He drank and he gambled and he screwed around."

Her parents' marriage was explosive from the start, and it ended in divorce when Maggie was eleven. As Maggie tells the story, her mother is the heroine. "In those days you didn't just pick up and leave with six kids to support. You stayed married for twenty-one years even if you were miserable."

Soon after the divorce, Maggie's father remarried and worked in his wife's beauty shop. He had more money then, but Maggie felt guilty about accepting his gifts, as though it would be disloyal to her mother. It was just the two of them now; Maggie's older siblings were all out of the house by the time she entered high school.

Just before her graduation, Maggie's father stopped paying child support. Her mother moved from the house the couple had shared into an apartment, her rent increasing while her income fell. Though Maggie had been thinking about attending Binghamton's Broome Community College to take nursing courses, she quickly abandoned the idea. She decided that she would stay with her mother and get a job to help pay the rent.

Her father offered to help her find a job, and this time Maggie accepted. A regular client at the beauty shop was a hiring manager for New York Telephone, then part of AT&T. Maggie's father gave the woman a bottle of scotch, and his daughter got the interview.

"AT&T was always a good job. I think I started out making $99.50 a week, and those were great wages. Of course, the job market around here was a lot better in 1971 than it is today. Back then, there were several big companies that were hiring. There was IBM, of course, and Singer Link, an aircraft manufacturer."

For several years, Maggie and her mother lived like companionable roommates. Her mother worked from seven in the morning to three-thirty in the afternoon, while Maggie drew the swing shift from two until ten o'clock at night, a schedule she has always preferred. Periodically Maggie thought about going to college, with her mother's encouragement, but she couldn't quite find the confidence. "I didn't know what to do with myself," she says. "So I stayed with the phone company."

As her mother had predicted, Maggie only left home when she got married. Her husband, Michael, was a local bartender, a good-looking man three years older than Maggie. They met in 1974, when Maggie was twenty, and married a year later. In the fall of 1977, when Michael decided he wanted to move to Florida, Maggie quit her job; she moved with her husband to St. Petersburg and found work as a hostess in a nightclub.

The marriage never stood a chance. After one especially stormy row, Maggie packed up her clothes, threw them into the back of her car—grateful that it was her own, bought with money saved from her days at AT&T—and drove back to Binghamton. Several months later, Michael turned up to discuss a reconciliation, but Maggie would not consider it. Her divorce was final within the year.

Maggie had no trouble getting her old operator job back, but she had to start over as a temporary employee. It was two and a half years before she was made a permanent staffer. Her time in Florida meant that she lost seniority—and as a result, for the next twenty years she could never take any of her four weeks' annual vacation past April. Co-workers with more service would always have first claim on the summer and fall dates.

An operator's job could be gratifying, but at times it was numbingly tedious. There was an inescapable indignity to the work. Operators were prohibited from talking to co-workers. Literally every minute had to be accounted for: if an operator had to go to the bathroom, she would raise her hand, and a supervisor would grant a "skip out."

At the same time, especially in her early years, Maggie and her fellow operators felt a personal connection to the customer and believed that they provided a valuable service. Operators laughed at the refrain of Lily Tomlin's character, Ernestine—"We don't care, we don't have to, we're the phone company"—but most of them, like Maggie, took pride in their own small domain. The job had a definite autonomy. "I liked being an operator," Maggie says. "Between 'AT&T, how can we help you?' and 'Thank you for using AT&T,' I was on my own."

Her career began in the final days of the "cord board." The board in Maggie's office was huge—about ten feet high and sixty feet wide, a vast expanse of holes and lights. Operators sat in rows, side by side. When the call began, the hole was empty and the light went on; when it ended, the hole was plugged and the light went out. Until about 1980, Maggie would manually record on IBM punch cards each long-distance call that she connected.

In the Binghamton office, which she joined in 1971, Maggie was one of about 350 operators. Long-distance operators sat at one end of a floor, and directory assistance was at the other. Through the late 1970s, Maggie covered a territory whose radius was just thirty miles, east from Binghamton to Hancock, New York. She and her coworkers recognized the voices of at least one in three customers.

In the early 1980s AT&T introduced a new computer system, called the Traffic Service Position System (TSPS), that expanded the reach of Maggie's office through the Syracuse area. The personal connection between operators and customers began to fray. When AT&T introduced a more sophisticated system a few years later, Maggie's office acquired all of upstate New York and parts of Connecticut. "Suddenly, we had 914, 315, 607, 518, and 716." She identifies the area codes in a respectful tone; the numbers are part of her personal history.

By then, of course, Maggie and her fellow operators rarely recognized voices on the other end of the line. Their work had become more impersonal and less autonomous. Intensifying this sense of alienation was an increasing pressure to work fast. Nothing else really mattered to management. "Before, you would give good service; you would try to help," Maggie says. "Now you had to get off the line as soon as possible. Thirty seconds was the goal."

Autonomy suddenly seemed a luxury to most operators: an emerging technology posed a direct threat to their jobs. In 1988 the CWA union learned that scientists at Bell Labs, the prestigious research arm of AT&T, were close to completing work on a new voice recognition technology. It made possible what has since become commonplace:

when a person dials directory assistance, he has a conversation with a machine.

As a CWA leader, Maggie joined the union's fight against the technology, but she was enough of a realist to know that the innovation could not be suppressed. She did hope it could somehow be contained, so that existing operator jobs could be saved.

Maggie's career as a union activist was born out of private indignation more than any public ambition. She was 19 years old and had been on the job for two years when her working relationship with one particular manager, strained from the outset, finally collapsed. The scene typifies the pettiness that pervaded AT&T bureaucracy.

"Back in the cord-board days," Maggie recalls, "they had these tall director chairs for the managers to sit on. From that perch they could look over at an operator's station and see how many phone calls she was fielding.

"So this manager walks over to tell me that I'm working too slowly. Later she came back to my position and, in the middle of a call, she closed my key—that's the instrument that allowed you to connect a call. She disconnected a customer just to yell at me. That was the final straw as far as I was concerned. No one is allowed to touch your position; that was a hard and fast company rule."

Maggie reported the incident to her union steward and was told that the matter would be taken care of. The next day, Maggie saw the union steward in an office with the manager and the chief operator. The manager denied the accusation, and "that was the end of the story. [I thought,] 'That's how they handle a situation like this?' I decided I would run for steward myself."

Maggie's union work gave her a new confidence. "I quickly realized that if I knew what I was talking about, people would listen to me," she says. When Maggie returned to AT&T after the breakup of her marriage, she learned that a member of the executive board of her union local had suddenly resigned. In the fall of 1988, Maggie was appointed to take her place.

Her first major union battle came in 1989, when operators for NYNEX, the old New York Telephone, went out on strike. After the breakup of the Bell System, Maggie had chosen to work at AT&T instead of one of the baby Bells. As a union leader, though, she felt obliged to join her fellow operators on the picket line. The strike lasted four months; the union paid Maggie for her meals and expenses during that time, but her salary was lost.

In retrospect, the more ominous development that year was the company edict that required operators to record on tape the phrase, "AT&T, how may I help you?" When a call came in, the operator would press a button, and the customer would hear her recorded greeting. "I had to play the tape, even though I was sitting right there and could have said the words myself. We all knew what this was about: the company was preparing the public for robots.

"The operators themselves were so afraid to buck the system," Maggie says, still baffled by the passivity of her coworkers. "They thought they were protecting their jobs by doing what the company wanted. They just refused to understand that this could mean the end of their livelihood."

In 1991 and 1992, the union organized informational picket lines to protest the new technology. "'Keep operators human. If you reach a robot, dial O," the placards read. The turnout was barely noticeable. On any given day, fewer than twenty operators would appear.

Maggie has a sense of history, and she understood that the steady assault of labor-saving technology had made America's telephone operators a dwindling breed for decades. The number of U.S. operators peaked at 262,000 in 1948; a few years later, new electro-mechanical switching systems made it possible to make direct long-distance calls for the first time. The operator—the human switch—became redundant.

Maggie has long had ambivalent feelings about technology. "Technology can be a force for the good, as I know from personal experience," she says. Her eldest brother, Jerry, died in 1979 of a brain tumor at the age of thirty-five, leaving a wife and three young children. The doctors had missed the diagnosis years before, and by the time they discovered the malignancy, the tumor could not be treated. An MRI might have saved his life.

Even so, Maggie was a reluctant convert when she and other AT&T operators began using computers in 1980. Her suspicions were painfully confirmed when she was diagnosed with carpal tunnel syndrome, which forced her out on disability for several months in 1993.

The power of the new technology in her own working life makes Maggie feel old at forty-two. "I don't want to become one of those people who gets older and can't accept any change," Maggie says, "because that's not who I am. I do think we're moving toward a two-tier society: obviously, the people who like the technology and keep up with it will be ahead of the people who don't. I'm not crazy about it, but it's here, and I know I can't resist it."

The old AT&T building where Maggie once worked stands empty now. It is a two-story brick building on Conklin Avenue, an ordinary street in a modest residential neighborhood. Across the road is Crowley's dairy ("It's Worth Crying Over," reads the sign on the roof), which has been selling milk in Binghamton since 1904.

AT&T had been shutting operator offices for years, and so it surprised no one when AT&T decreed that the Binghamton office would be closed for good in June 1994. But even though employees had about six months' notice, they ignored the inevitable, believing (in the face of all reason) that the company would never go through with it. As the final date approached, the most inconsequential disputes would escalate into angry arguments—feeling betrayed by the company, people turned on each other. During these final months, Maggie herself was out on disability: her carpal tunnel had flared up, and doctors told her not to do any work.

AT&T gave its employees the option of applying to transfer to one of its remaining operator offices, and Maggie might have tried to relocate to Norfolk, Virginia. At the time, though, her mother was dying, and she could not contemplate a move.

Parenthetically, operators did appreciate one irony of their plight. Thanks to their union, operators were actually better off than their bosses in terms of their severance pay. A forty-year-old hourly worker with ten years' service, for example, walked away with twenty weeks of termination pay, versus fifteen weeks for a manager with the same tenure.

What's more, only hourly workers escaped a penalty for retiring before they turned fifty-five. In 1994, for instance, a fifty-year-old operator with thirty years' service would be entitled to a monthly pension of $787, plus a $52,850 termination payment. A manager near the bottom of the corporate ladder would receive a larger monthly pension payment ($1,391) but a much smaller termination payment ($34,228).

Gerry Nelson was a human resources manager whose territory included all of the operator offices in upstate New York. Maggie and her fellow operators cheered Gerry on as she waged a spirited but futile campaign to shame AT&T into giving comparable severance packages to its managers. Because this would have easily cost the company tens of millions of dollars, however, Gerry never had a chance.

Unlike many of her colleagues, Gerry could afford to retire. With thirty-five years of service, she would suffer only a slight discount on her pension based on her age (she was fifty-three years old) when she left the company. Nevertheless, Gerry organized managers to write ten thousand letters to the company chairman. She also orchestrated conference calls with human resources executives who might have supported her cause.

At the annual stockholders meeting in Atlanta, she addressed the company's chairman, Bob Allen: "I am here representing approximately five hundred managers regarding AT&T's decision not to offer any additional pension options, at a time when AT&T is going through a devastating downsizing. . . . We trusted AT&T'S leadership and trusted that you would care for us. Bob, you have failed us."

Gerry requested a meeting with Allen, but she was refused. Determined to see the AT&T chairman "eye to eye," she took a seat in the lobby of a Manhattan building on the morning of a scheduled board meeting. When Allen appeared, Gerry introduced herself. "I told him that I just wanted to meet him face to face. He looked at me for just a second, and it was as though I were transparent. He shook my hand, and then he walked away."

"Gerry went to bat for her people, though she would gain nothing by it," Maggie says. "Of course, the system was stacked against her."

So, unemployed, Maggie found herself caught in the downdraft of the most severe corporate downsizing in U.S. history: IBM's slashing of 60,000 jobs from its payroll in 1993. Like AT&T, the old IBM had all but guaranteed lifetime employment, and over the years most of upstate New York had grown far too dependent on IBM jobs and tax revenue. When the computer giant pulled back, these local economies went into a tailspin. As a result, in closing its Binghamton office, AT&T threw its downsized workers into a very bleak job market.

With considerable energy but minimal expectations, Maggie began to look for work. She certainly had the qualifications to earn more than the minimum wage. At AT&T's expense, she had gone back to school and earned an associate's degree and paralegal certificate (with a 3.8 grade point average) from Broome Community College. Since much of her union responsibility had revolved around the language of the CWA contract, paralegal work seemed a sensible choice.

In upstate New York, though, legal work was scarce—especially for someone like Maggie, who had little on-the-job experience. Through an employment agency, she took what work she could get, making six dollars an hour answering the phone, filing papers, and typing forms in an insurance claims office. Her best job paid eight dollars an hour; in it, she stood in a BP gas station, asking customers to sign up for a new Visa card.

"Working at AT&T from the age of seventeen to forty," Maggie says, "it never occurred to me that you might quit a job just because you didn't like it at any given moment. But with temp work, the fact is that if some boss is hassling you, you can just pick yourself up and walk out the door. I never quite got used to that."

As her debts mounted and her savings dwindled—and she reluctantly took another temp assignment that paid six dollars an hour—Maggie began to feel herself slipping. AT&T had given a middle-class income. Where was she now?

Though she appreciated that the phone company had always provided a good wage, Maggie never assumed any social status from her paycheck. It had offended her to see AT&T salespeople—men and women who were paid only a few thousand dollars a year more than she was—flaunt their superior rank. She feels that most of us are two, maybe three steps from serious financial hardship. "Status doesn't help you when they come to foreclose on your house," she says.

When she learned about the AT&T opening in Syracuse, Maggie accepted its inevitability. "I'm going out there because it is desperate in Binghamton right now. I have to keep things in perspective. I was not able to find a job at anywhere near this pay. I have six more years—six more years—before I can claim my pension." Her new relationship with AT&T is, essentially, a business transaction.

Arriving to take the qualifying test, Maggie spotted several familiar faces, fellow operators from across upstate New York. A written exam lasted about an hour. "They gave you two lists of mostly identical names," Maggie recalls, "and you had to spot the slight differences: Joan Smith and Jean Smith, say. Or there were two lists of numbers, and you had to notice the change from 4561 to 4651. It was vaguely annoying, but not hard."

Credited for her past years of service with AT&T, Maggie's starting salary jumped from the minimum $369 to $542 per week. Like many of her colleagues, Maggie began as a temporary, or "term," employee. AT&T guaranteed her job for at least a year, possibly three years. At that point, term status would end. AT&T would either hire the employee as a full-time staffer or end the assignment.

This division of AT&T, like many others, was pushing for a more flexible workforce. Hiring term employees was an obvious solution to uncertain demand. The system was clearly beneficial to the company, and employees were in no position to complain.

Before Maggie arrived, the Syracuse office had been on a hiring spree for more than a year following a reorganization of AT&T's basic customer service organization. The restructuring was one piece of the company's "one-stop shopping" strategy. To encourage customers to use AT&T for all their communication needs—local, long distance, wireless, and private data lines—AT&T set up new "customer care" centers that allow AT&T's business customers to call one office to solve any problems or answer any questions.

In 1996, Dave Burns, the AT&T veteran in charge of the Syracuse office, hired one hundred term employees. By the start of 1997, fifty-eight of these workers, including Maggie, had been promoted to the regular staff.

For Maggie, the change was dramatic; her twenty-two years of service will now protect her during the next downsizing. AT&T's contract with the union dictates that any layoff of occupational workers respect seniority: the last hired are the first fired. As long as the entire office is not closed down—it could happen, of course, but at the moment it seems an unlikely prospect—Maggie should be able to hang on.

Maggie sits at an L-shaped desk that she shares with a coworker. One long shelf is filled with office manuals, plus framed photographs of her three nieces and nephews and her two dogs. A half-gallon plastic container is usually filled with diet soda. Maggie's seniority gives her a window that looks out on a courtyard. "Twenty-two years has to be good for something," she says with a laugh.

Maggie works as one of five members of a team that handles the account of a Fortune 500 company. They respond to queries and requests from the AT&T sales force responsible for large corporate customers.

On a typical morning, Maggie receives a thirty-page fax from an AT&T account executive. Company X, which spends millions of dollars a year with AT&T, has acquired a new subsidiary, whose network of phone and fax lines must be absorbed into Company X's system. First, Maggie must "scrub" each phone number—is it a legitimate number? If not, is a new line needed? In the latter case, the local phone company must be contacted. If the number is accurate, Maggie enters the data into the AT&T network and billing system. Then it's on to the next number.

She worried about the physical demands of the position. From eight in the morning to four in the afternoon, she sits in front of a computer, taking two fifteen-minute breaks and a half hour for lunch. Maggie knew that the job would exacerbate the strain in her shoulder and probably aggravate her carpal tunnel syndrome as well. As if to confirm her fears, after six months her back went out and she was home on disability leave for five weeks. When Maggie returned, though, she felt much better, and she feels fairly confident that she will be able to do her job.

The constant petty indignities of the operator's job have disappeared, and for that Maggie is grateful. "I have much more freedom now. Just the ability to stand up and walk to the bathroom when you feel like it is something I appreciate. In the Binghamton office, the rule was that only one operator could leave her position at any given time. We had a system where we took a pole in the center of the room and put a hat on it. When you went to the bathroom, you took the hat off the pole, and when you returned, you put it back on. That's how the supervisor knew if she could call the next person in line.

"It was kindergarten stuff. But there you are."

She also makes considerably more money now. In her best year as an operator, she says, she earned $34,000 (with "tons and tons of overtime"), but she generally averaged about $28,000 a year. After twelve months in her new job, she will receive top pay of $751 a week, or more than $39,000 a year.

Her new salary and job title give Maggie a greater status within the organization, and her identity has changed along with it. Maggie has not yet sorted out the substance of this shift. Talking about it, her voice—normally self-confident—becomes softer and more tentative. It is clearly a sensitive subject.

"Before, I'd say to people, 'I'm an operator.' Now I'm not exactly sure what I am," Maggie says. "It's not something I focus on. But there is a class distinction between us and the operators . . . this perception that we are superior. Well, we are paid more. But that doesn't make me feel any better." The last thing Maggie wants to do is imitate the snobbery of the salespeople in her old office.

Though her new job demands more of her intelligence than her old one, it is can also be more alienating. As an operator, Maggie was a disembodied voice saying "Thank you for using AT&T" over and over again. But she made a direct connection to the customer and, like many veteran operators, found a distinct satisfaction in providing a simple service.

Her new working identity is more amorphous. Entering addresses into a data bank so that a subsidiary of a subsidiary of a major corporation can set up a new network . . . is also customer service, but it is far removed from talking to an actual person and connecting a call.

As an operator, Maggie could feel a personal tie to the heritage of this historic company. AT&T, after all, was built on the labor and the spirit of its operators. Though her status in the organization was lower when she was an operator, in a sense she felt more valuable.

For the moment, Maggie is focusing on learning all the quirks of her new job. "At this point I feel like I've been given pieces of the puzzle, and I don't know exactly where they all fit. Maybe some day they'll come together." She takes pride in her work, and she is determined to recapture what she took for granted as an operator—an unchallenged mastery of the system. She knew the job cold, and that felt good.

An important part of Maggie's old identity as an operator was defined by her leadership position in the Communications Workers of America union. Though she supports the union, and keeps an eye on its administration, for now Maggie has no plans to run for office. "That time has passed," she says.

She still misses the camaraderie of her old operator offices, where many people worked together for ten or twenty years. "I grew up in this job," Maggie says. While the vast majority of her Binghamton coworkers were middle-aged women, Maggie now finds herself surrounded by twenty-three-year-olds. "I'm closer in age to their mothers!" Maggie says, unable to take herself too seriously for any length of time.

Maggie believes that economic forces drove her out of AT&T, and economic forces pulled her back into the fold. The company fired operators because they could; Maggie came back because she had to.

That will only change, Maggie is convinced, when society's resources are more justly distributed. "America is increasingly polarized between the haves and have-nots," Maggie says. "Where will it all end?

Sometimes I think it's just all greed and the mighty buck. How much money, how much profit is enough?" Then her indignation subsides, and pragmatism prevails. "I can put up with just about anything for six years, knowing I'll have a guaranteed pension and benefits," Maggie says.

A fitting postscript: a year after Maggie started working in AT&T's Syracuse office, she quit her job to take a new one at NYNEX—the old New York Telephone when it was part of the AT&T empire, and Maggie's first employer. The company's pact with the CWA union states that Maggie's pension is "portable," which means that her seniority and benefits remain intact. In fact, top pay in her new position as a residential customer service representative will be thirty-five dollars a week more than she earned at AT&T. The work itself is quite similar, though now she deals with residential rather than corporate customers. For Maggie, though, the main appeal of the NYNEX job is its location: her office is now a five-minute drive from her house.

When Maggie reported to her new job, she walked into the same building where she had worked twenty-six years ago, as a seventeen-year-old operator straight out of school. "Back then you had to go up one step to get into the building," she says. "It's since been paved to make [it] wheelchair accessible. But for a while I found myself picking up my foot, looking for the step that isn't there."

In the spring of 1997, when Maggie began at NYNEX, the company was very close to completing its merger with Bell Atlantic, another baby Bell. The combined phone company, now called Bell Atlantic, will fight AT&T for customers and profits, as Maggie well knows. "Who can say whether Bell Atlantic or AT&T will be the safer place to work? It's a toss of the coin."

Perhaps her new employer will begin downsizing in upstate New York. If Maggie has to relocate, though, this time she will. She wants to hang on: in the year 2003, she will make her thirty years.

7   KYLE STEVENS

The certificate was embossed with an illustration of "Golden Boy," the twenty-four-foot-tall statue symbolizing the "spirit of communication" that has stood sentry at AT&T headquarters since 1914. It was signed by Robert E. Allen, chairman and chief executive officer of AT&T. There was just one problem: Kyle had been fired three months earlier. He never quite reached that career milestone.

For Kyle this was more than a bureaucratic blunder: It was a powerful symbol. AT&T had been a critical part of his life for fourteen years. It had been a crucial part of his identity. But the company never knew who he was.

So be it, he said to himself. *Move on.*

Kyle Stevens (the name is a pseudonym at his request) was laid off from AT&T during the downsizing of 1996, amid the fury of the company's announced 40,000 job cuts. Quickly he shed his identity as an acquiescent, conscientious corporate foot soldier.

Returning to the company fold four months later, he was sobered and suspicious, a new kind of organization man. He had been hired as an independent contractor for a small consulting firm to work exclusively for NCR, the former Global Information Solutions division of AT&T until it was spun off as part of the breakup of the company. Kyle would join an NCR consulting team that had just signed a lucrative deal to work on a high-profile technology project for a major telecommunications company. The client, ironically, was AT&T.

Were the upheavals of the past year all just a game of musical chairs? Kyle still toils for the greater glory of AT&T, only now from a different perch. There is a new corporate logo on his paycheck. Other than that, on the surface it seems that little has changed.

Kyle, however, has changed. Once he secretly believed in "thirty years and a gold watch," as his childhood friend Tony Green has told him, but no more. He willfully purged from his vocabulary words he now thought archaic: *security*, *safety*, and the one he found quaintest of all, *loyalty*.

A tall, good-looking black man whose preppy style tends toward chinos and moccasins, Kyle is serious and straitlaced. A certain reserve never leaves him. During his fourteen-year career at AT&T, his calm, deliberate manner served him well. He was one of those quintessential team players who fill the middle layers of a large bureaucracy.

"What's in it for me? That's my new ideology," Kyle says. "I am not looking for a job that will make me, quote, more secure," Kyle says. "I don't believe in it and I won't fool myself into thinking that it exists. Any job I take, I'm going to ask, 'What is this doing for me now? Does it make sense for me to stay?' And if it doesn't, I will move, fast."

Kyle began to reconstruct his identity as a loyal company man suddenly, and in a state of shock. When he returned home after his last day at AT&T, March 15th, he learned that his eighty-three-year-old father had died that morning.

"What are the odds that this could happen, and on the Ides of March? The stars only line up like this once every ten thousand years," Kyle says. "It seemed significant, as if there were a lesson in it. It was time to turn the page."

Kyle grew up in a quiet town on the Jersey shore, in a house just five blocks from the beach. Strangely, neither he nor his six siblings were ever taught how to swim. Their parents were neither poor nor phobic; they were simply disinterested in their children's lives.

A talented athlete, Kyle played basketball and soccer throughout junior and senior high school. In the close-knit community, families would walk together to the games, but Kyle's parents never once appeared. "I wished that they had shown an interest," he says simply, "but I got the message: 'Hey, you're on your own.'"

Bob, Kyle's father, worked for thirty years as a planner in the nearby Earle naval station. Often he would erupt in stinging, demeaning attacks on one of his sons, though Kyle was spared the worst of these outbursts. "My father called the shots," Kyle says. "He was the breadwinner, he set the rules, things happened around him." Daisy, his mother, was a petite woman who invariably deferred to her husband. Though she gave birth to seven children over twenty years, Kyle says, she seemed to find little joy in being a mother.

While the navy paid a good wage, the household was in a chronic state of chaos. It was at best a haphazard sort of parenting: on Christmas Eve, the children would be taken to the local Sears an hour before the store closed.

There was an ingrained family legacy that Kyle would struggle to shake off, a conviction that the world is a dangerous place. "My parents believed you should keep your head down. Don't let people know anything about you, because if you do, you'll be vulnerable." Kyle's wife, Jan—a clinical psychologist as delightfully blunt as she is shrewd—was instantly struck by the family's negativism. "They can find something wrong in the fact that the sun rises and sets every day," she says with a laugh.

It was not an environment that inspired confidence or independence. It was a difficult world to escape, but Kyle did escape. He was the only son who did not follow his father's directive and join the armed forces. He was also the only one to earn a college degree (he went further and got an MBA). He was the only one who managed, finally, to move on.

As he considers the patterns of his life and the rhythm of his career, Kyle now sees that in leaving AT&T he recovered the self-determination and the courage to be his own man. In early middle age, he revived the rebellious youth who was hungry for adventure and eager to take a risk.

That independent spirit was slow to emerge. As Kyle drifted through high school, several teachers, recognizing his potential, spotted a classic underachiever. "I never had any problems," Kyle says, "but I never went after an A, either." He was shy, eager to stay out of trouble—confident only of his athletic skill. But his classmates knew him to be one of the brightest students in his grade, and they were surprised when Kyle chose to attend a community college.

"When I graduated from high school, I knew I didn't want to go into the service like my brothers, but that was all I knew," Kyle says. Avoiding the military was an important rejection of the established family pattern, as was Kyle's sudden refusal to join his father and brothers in hunting rabbit, duck, and the occasional deer in the dank New Jersey woodlands. "One day," Kyle recalls with a wan smile, "I realized that I didn't need to hunt these animals. It gave me no pleasure, so I just stopped. That was very perplexing to my family."

Kyle symbolically escaped underwater by becoming an accomplished scuba diver. "It takes you out of the world," he says. "You're weightless, every movement you make is completely effortless. You're in this impossibly beautiful environment [that is just] teeming with life."

When he defied his father by accepting an athletic and academic scholarship to Pace University at the age of twenty Kyle broke completely from his family's narrow world. On the anonymous New York City campus in the shadow of the Brooklyn Bridge, he came into his own.

New York was intimidating at first, but before long Kyle was intoxicated by the city. He would take afternoon runs in Central Park and meander through Greenwich Village in the evening. Majoring in business administration, he discovered that he had a particular affinity for computers. To earn some extra income, he took a part-time job as a COBOL computer programmer for one of the city's transit authorities.

At Pace, Kyle met the woman who would become his first wife. She was prim and slender, bearing more than a passing resemblance to his mother. Though Kyle had been in several casual relationships with women, this was his first serious romance. "They were a handsome couple," says Kyle's old friend Adrien. "They'd go on vacation and come back with pretty pictures. But the intimacy between them was shallow." They had dated for about two years when Kyle proposed, and in 1983 they married. Three years later the marriage fell apart and Kyle filed for divorce.

Two years after his divorce became final, Kyle met Jan. Trained as a clinical psychologist, Jan now works as a corporate consultant specializing in organizational development. As forthright as Kyle is reserved, Jan has gently nudged her husband to become more open.

The dynamic between them partly reflects their different life experiences. Although they are both African-American and grew up in large families, Jan was raised in a middle-class household in Dallas, the youngest daughter of two loving and supportive parents. When she was eight, her father died of heart failure at the age of forty. In the moment that her mother told her the news, Jan instinctively understood that the world had become a different place. "Not long after my father died," Jan says, "I remember thinking, 'One of these days Mom might not come back. I'm either going to make it or I'm not.' That is how I've lived my life."

She and Kyle met in the spring of 1989, when he was thirty-five and she was thirty-three. It was a blind date arranged by mutual friends, and neither of them arrived with any expectations of romance. Jan imagined that Kyle would be a smooth corporate operator, and Kyle expected a smug intellectual. They were both delighted to be instantly proven wrong. After dinner, as they were riding down an escalator, Jan tripped, and Kyle grabbed her elbow. "I'll never let you fall," he said.

Things moved quickly after that. Kyle and Jan became engaged six months later and married in July 1990, a little more than a year after that first date. In 1994 Jan gave birth to their son, David.

By the time Jan met Kyle, he was in the middle of his career at AT&T, and Jan quickly sensed the compromises and limitations he had come to accept.

The early years of his career, by contrast, had been charmed. Toward the end of his senior year in college, while most of his classmates were trudging through the help-wanted ads, Kyle relaxed: months earlier, a former Pace graduate student had recommended him to a mid-sized computer firm that specialized in applications software. The company had agreed to hire Kyle as a systems representative, where he would help design new systems for corporate clients. He graduated from Pace on a Friday and reported to work the next Monday.

About three years later, a headhunter called. Would Kyle be interested in getting into the telecommunications industry? There was an opening at AT&T that he might fill perfectly, and it promised a 40 percent raise. Without hesitating, Kyle accepted.

At the time, this was a symbolic leap in stature for a young black man who grew up in a working-class town on the Jersey shore. To his parents, Kyle recalls, AT&T was the perfect emblem of the "white Establishment"; to Kyle himself, it represented the pinnacle of corporate power. "I thought that once I was accepted in corporate America in a professional position, I would have arrived," Kyle says. "I believed that the opportunities would be endless, if I just worked hard and kept my nose to the grindstone."

In August 1981, Kyle glanced up at the shining statue of Golden Boy as he entered AT&T's headquarters for the first time. He began as a second-level manager and soon moved into what would prove to be his natural forte, product management. Product managers examine a specific marketplace, determine what kind of product or service to provide, and help coordinate the process of bringing it to market. The job capitalized on Kyle's ability to make a considered analysis of a business situation. His even temperament proved useful in dealing with the rival corporate constituencies—techies, marketers, and salesmen—who join the development process at one stage or another. One needs patience and self-control to keep the egos in check.

Kyle performed well, and his talents were quickly appreciated. At the age of twenty-nine, he was promoted to district manager, a step in the corporate ladder that most AT&T managers do not reach until their mid-thirties. He was on his way.

Almost imperceptibly, the resourceful, self-confident young manager evolved into a company man who sacrificed too much for a safety that proved to be illusory.

His jobs at AT&T were varied and challenging, and they lulled Kyle into a sense that he was moving forward rather than just around the sprawling organization. Like many large companies, AT&T gives its employees the chance to develop a range of skills in different business units; Kyle exploited those opportunities, always receiving above-average performance evaluations. For one reason or another, though—bad timing, political forces in the organization that were beyond his control—a promotion to division manager (the next level in the hierarchy) did not come.

Bureaucracies inspire a pervasive sense that "they" have a master plan for your career. But, as Kyle would come to see with painful clarity, there is no "they"—only a revolving door of men and women in a series of shifting alliances whose governing rules are similarly in flux. In such an environment, what seem to be sensible, self-protective judgments about the future often turn out to be based on assumptions that no longer apply. That is what happened to Kyle, again and again.

At the time of his early promotion to district manager in 1984, Kyle was (in the vernacular) "supervising the product delivery" of the X.25 series of private data networking equipment. AT&T management hoped that this product might help it set a triumphant high-tech course following the breakup of the Bell System. But after studying the economics of the business, Kyle's boss determined that AT&T would not be able to make a go of it, and she closed down the division in 1987.

Along with his colleagues on the X.25 team, Kyle looked for a new assignment. By now, Bob Allen and his deputies were eagerly pursuing their dream of conquering the computer industry. Kyle had experience in the software business, and in the wake of his recent setback, he thought it made sense to use it. "I thought I should go back to something I knew, and I knew software pretty well."

He took a job managing a small group in the computer division. Under Kyle's leadership, the group's product documentation system was transformed from an obvious liability into a recognized industry standard. Cost-cutting is one sure way to get management's attention, and Kyle succeeded in this when he took charge of a distribution and inventory control team that saved the division more than $3 million.

As things played out, however, these accomplishments proved of limited value within AT&T. Bob Allen's disastrous 1991 decision to buy the NCR Corporation made many AT&T departments suddenly obsolete. It took only three months for Kyle's group to be shut down; he was one of the thousands of AT&T employees who found themselves unexpected casualties of the merger.

This might have been a moment to look for work outside the comfortable borders of AT&T, but once again Kyle finessed a smooth transfer by moving out of computers and into consumer services. This was the core division of AT&T, whose main business was providing long-distance phone service for residential customers.

AT&T is such a far-flung organization that Kyle could almost pretend that he was working for a different company. His new assignment represented a real change. As a district manager in new business development, Kyle gained authority, managing a department of twenty-four people whose mission was to identify potential new consumer businesses.

It is a rare moment when a middle manager in a corporate hierarchy can point to something—a product, a program, or even an idea—and say, "That's mine." Kyle's chance came when he launched and directed a quarterly series of business development seminars that attracted about one hundred managers from different business units within AT&T, people whose paths would not normally cross. In bringing them together, the forum enabled disparate groups to share market research and explore ideas for new businesses. "Everyone loved it, they kept coming back. That was my creation," says Kyle with palpable pride.

This success helped Kyle snare his most high-profile job at AT&T, as the executive assistant to a president. The title carried real status in the organization, especially if one's boss was well-placed in the firmament—in the way of all bureaucracies, access to power *is* power. Kyle's boss was a substantial figure at AT&T, having scored a great success as the creator of the company's Universal credit card. Since Kyle had reached a plateau at the district manager level, this position held out the promise of energizing his career.

When Kyle came to work for him, this president was running the company's multimedia strategy group. (*Interactive* and *multimedia* have since lost their luster, but they were the industry buzzwords of the day.) Kyle joined a group of less than a dozen people charged with defining AT&T's approach to multimedia, then "migrating" that strategy into specific business units. In other words, they needed to persuade the guys on the line to make good on their lofty ideas. That process required a delicate combination of deference and forceful persuasion, and Kyle's natural tact—as well as his instinctive ability to forge a consensus—proved an asset here.

"As an executive assistant, you need good management skills and good interpersonal skills," says Doug Dunn. Dunn served as an AT&T vice president and the number two executive in multimedia strategy before leaving the company in 1996 to become dean of Carnegie Mellon's business school. Kyle did the job well, he says. "He's a substantive person. He was not aggressive or pushy. The more you got to know him, the more you respected him."

The group's president respected Kyle too, but he was not about to confide in him or anyone else on the team. As a result, Kyle and his colleagues were all taken aback in the spring of 1994 when this president announced that he was retiring from AT&T to work for a start-up company.

Kyle had just begun to think about what his next move might be when he got a call from the office of a senior executive in Network Systems. (This was AT&T's equipment division—originally Western Electric, which was later spun off as Lucent Technologies as part of the 1996 breakup of the company.) Perhaps Kyle would be interested in taking a strategy job?

"Network Systems had something of a reputation of being less open to women and blacks," Dunn recalls, but he nonetheless advised Kyle to take the position. He thought the corporate culture had changed enough that Kyle could do well there.

Kyle was apprehensive, but he also wanted to stay in the corporate cocoon. Kyle recounts his thinking at the time: "There weren't many openings in the services group, which was going through a downsizing that year. And I said to myself, 'Well, I've been at the district manager level for nine years, and it hasn't been easy to move up. Maybe what I need to do is increase my portfolio of skills.' I had never worked in Network Systems before, and I told myself it would be a growth experience."

The voice of a rebellious youth had been stilled. In its place was the spirit of middle-aged stagnation.

Periodically in recent years, and specifically at this juncture, Kyle's wife encouraged her husband to think about leaving AT&T. "I knew people would interpret the fact that he hadn't further advanced as a comment on his talent and abilities. I thought his career would flourish elsewhere. But Kyle always felt compelled to defend the company."

Kyle had been knocked about by the corporate winds—a business shut down, a division reorganized, a boss suddenly quitting—but one way or another, he had never lost his footing.

A year and a half later, though, when AT&T decreed that 40,000 jobs would be cut as part of the company's breakup and Kyle was among those declared "at risk," he looked back upon this last move as the decisive blunder of his AT&T career. When layoff time arrived in Network Systems, a basic pattern prevailed. The division's veterans held on, and many of the newcomers to the division—even those with decades of experience elsewhere at AT&T—fell to the ground.

Minutes after the breakup was announced, AT&T employees began to speculate about how deep the inevitable downsizing would go. It seemed a safe bet that few divisions would be immune.

In his 13 months in his new job, Kyle realized that he had underestimated the gulf between the corporate culture of Network Systems and the Consumer and Computer Divisions where he had spent his entire AT&T career. The old Western Electric sensibility at Network Systems—the engineer's devotion to rigid procedures, the inbred organization that views outsiders with suspicion—was very much alive. "There was a siege mentality there," says one of Kyle's colleagues, another new-comer. "They didn't trust people outside the fold."

The substance of Kyle's work had also changed. Though his new job as a strategist drew upon his established talents in analyzing markets and identifying business opportunities, he had only cursory knowledge of the group's basic product line. It took time to learn all that he needed to know.

Finally and ominously, Kyle had a frosty relationship with his boss's boss—the group's vice president, the most important figure in the land-scape when any downsizing began. This is the man who would ulti-mately determine which employees would be branded "at risk."

After feeling the first pangs of panic, Kyle received surprisingly good news: AT&T was sending him off to a three-week program at the Thunderbird School of International Management in Arizona, an edu-cational retreat for managers at mid-career. *Would they send me off on this nice little jaunt,* Kyle asked himself, *if they were planning to get rid of me? They must see me as one of the survivors.*

It was a precarious faith, shared by so many organization men at companies like AT&T, that the company was a cohesive entity making rational, predictable judgments. The reality was much more random.

Tony Green talked with his old friend when the layoffs were threat-ened but not yet announced, and he could hear the undercurrent of fear beneath Kyle's outward calm. "He was getting tense. But when they sent him off to the management school, he thought, 'You don't do this without having plans for me.' It was a great relief, you could hear it in his voice. I think that's why he was so shocked when they actually laid him off."

Unlike Kyle, Jan grew fearful the moment she learned of the com-pany breakup and the layoffs that were sure to follow. "The handwriting was on the wall," she recalls. "Kyle had been in his new organization for only a short while. His boss was a problem. His group was not part of any line operation. I had a strong suspicion that this time Kyle would take the hit."

Jan's instincts proved astute; the strategy groups in Network Systems were particularly vulnerable. Company guidelines may be written to inspire justice and fair play, but selecting layoff victims is by definition a subjective process. At Network Systems, the old-timers were seen to take care of their own. Newcomers—even if they had spent twenty years working at AT&T—were at a definite disadvantage in looking for a new job within the division.

Kyle believed that since minorities had only recently been recruited into the strategy groups of Network Systems, they were disproportionately represented among the division's newcomers. In his own twenty-person strategy group, Kyle was one of four minority employees, all of whom had been asked to join the division within about a year of the downsizing. "It's not like I applied," says one of Kyle's former colleagues. "They came knocking at my door." All four of them were placed "at risk" during the 1996 downsizing. One retired; two found AT&T jobs outside the division. Without addressing the specifics of any case, an AT&T spokesman says that careful attention was given to ensure that no racial or ethnic group was unfairly affected by downsizing.

Once he was "at risk," Kyle had only the mandated sixty days to find a new job within AT&T, yet he remained sanguine. Though he had never been formally declared at risk before, Kyle had been forced to find a new position in the company on four previous occasions, and something had always turned up. "I've been through this before," Kyle thought, "I'll get through it again." After fourteen years with the company, Kyle had cocooned himself in an illusion of safety.

His wife urged Kyle to use the data bank at AT&T's outplacement center in Murray Hill to look for a new job. Like many of his unlucky colleagues, though, Kyle focused almost exclusively on potential opportunities within AT&T. That felt like the comfortable thing to do. He made only perfunctory attempts to pursue outside leads.

"Are you really looking outside?" Jan would ask Kyle during this period.

"Yes, yes," would be the reply.

"Who have you contacted, what have you done?" Jan insisted.

Not much, was the honest answer.

"I had been fired once," Jan says, "I knew what was in store for Kyle if he didn't find a job soon."

Kyle did come within a whisker of surviving the downsizing. (He later found it ironic that the trumpeted 40,000 job cuts did not come to pass, as many of those placed "at risk" managed to find new positions.)

His last hope appeared through some old friends in the consumer services group, who told him of an opening in AT&T's on-line division, which would later be known as WorldNet. The group planned to develop several online offerings; Kyle had the right experience and qualifications, and he impressed the executives he met. Over the course of three weeks, they called Kyle in for four different interviews. Finally they offered him a job, which he quickly accepted.

Still, bureaucracies respect their own particular codes, and Kyle knew that he would not be safe until a piece of paper said so. "Come back on February 15th," they told him, "and we will sign the necessary forms." But late in the day on February 13th, Kyle got a phone call. The manager was contrite. The word had just come down: AT&T was scrapping some of its online ventures; a hiring freeze was now in effect. Kyle's job offer was hereby rescinded. "Good luck," the manager added, and then he hung up.

When his last day arrived, Kyle felt an unexpected peace. "I got up around 6:30, and I went to work." He catches himself and laughs. "I went to the office at 8:30. I still had some packing left to do, and there was a job lead or two I thought I might hear about, but I didn't."

Two coworkers in his small group had only recently found jobs within AT&T. The two men kept dropping by Kyle's office under various pretexts, doing their best to bolster his spirits. Kyle gave them a few office items he wanted to pass along—a good desk pad, and a high-end computer. "Take them now," Kyle said. "Don't let someone else grab them."

Kyle called a porter—a parting corporate perk—and then went to the parking lot to get his car. Glancing up at the office windows, he noticed a colleague looking at him. Yes, Kyle said to himself, *I'm one of the ones who didn't make it.*

He had been home for a few hours when his brother Dave called. Their father had died of a heart attack at 6:30 that morning. The funeral would be held in three days.

That his family had waited eight hours before anyone thought to deliver the news was a further reminder of how estranged Kyle was from his family. He himself had told none of them about the downsizing. Kyle thought he might not even mention it to his older brother, but let it slip toward the end of their brief conversation. Kyle accepted his brother's sympathy, then quickly changed the subject.

The rest of the evening passed in a haze. Though Kyle's father was eighty-three when he died, he had been in reasonably good health, and his death came as a shock. After several weeks, Kyle began to absorb the loss. "I had come to terms with the relationship in recent years. When my father died, the sorrow that I felt was for a loss of hope, the hope that I might have had a different kind of relationship with him."

Although it is purely a coincidence that both Kyle and Vincent Smith found themselves unemployed at the same time that they were mourning the death of a father, it is not surprising that they each perceived the layoff in familial terms. His sense of what it means to be a man—a working man, a family man, a provider—naturally begins with a father's example. For Kyle, it was an example that he both rejected and in some ways repeated.

His father had no ambition for himself beyond serving out his time in the naval yards at Earle. For his sons, he held no grander aspirations. College was a pointless indulgence; the military would do just fine.

Kyle defied those presumptions most dramatically when he arrived at Pace University, and again when he joined AT&T. In his career, he surpassed anything his parents had ever imagined for him. The only time Kyle and his father talked about his work at AT&T, though, was when Kyle received his promotion to executive assistant. Feeling both proud and envious of his son's success, his father responded by relaying the news of a childhood friend who had recently moved up to foreman.

If Kyle had left AT&T even two years earlier than he did, his story would be quite different. But as he lingered too long in the company's clasp—soothing at first, suffocating at the last—he became a Fortune 500 version of his father, the middle manager's equivalent of the thirty-year navy man.

"Kyle was secretly looking for a safe haven," says Jan. "He broke away from his family, but in many ways he kept looking for predictability and stability. Once he settled into AT&T, he allowed himself to feel protected." In the end, Kyle found a repetition of what he had experienced in his family: the illusion of security, but never the thing itself.

His identity as an unreconstructed company man peeled away with surprising speed. "It was just a few weeks after the layoff that I had this tremendous sense of relief. I was still anxious about finding a new job, but I had this realization—'I don't have to play this game anymore, being the good employee and believing that if I do the right thing, I'll be rewarded.'"

It was restorative for Kyle to see himself as others did, as a valuable commodity in the job market. He had diverse and solid experience in telecommunications and computing technology, and he was articulate and personable. Once he seriously began to search for a new job, Kyle was fielding numerous calls from headhunters and receiving a steady stream of plausible job prospects. Almost always he was called in for an interview.

Outplacement advisers, though, routinely say that the best way to find a new job is through a personal connection. So, calling up phone numbers he had not dialed in years, Kyle got in touch with former colleagues from his days in the computer group of AT&T. They were now well-placed in the NCR hierarchy. Delivering a now well-honed speech, Kyle asked if they knew of any leads in the industry. They immediately told Kyle about open positions at NCR for which he would be well qualified.

Through all the AT&T downsizings, Kyle recalls, he heard the same refrain: "Don't worry, even if you get laid off, you can always come back as a consultant." This was easiest for a senior executive to arrange, but many middle managers cobbled together similar (though less lucrative) arrangements.

Since NCR was a former division of AT&T, though, Kyle would be forced to return whatever remained of his severance package if he began working there within six months of leaving the AT&T payroll. Kyle was loath to do this; he wanted the money, and he felt that he deserved it. *Let them make me a job offer first*, Kyle thought to himself, *and then we'll see.*

In the middle of his interview with a human resources manager at NCR, the perfect solution presented itself. Kyle could work as an independent contractor for a consulting firm that had an arrangement with NCR. Kyle's paycheck would come from the consulting firm, as would his insurance coverage (the job would include decent benefits, he was assured). Kyle would be working full-time for NCR, but technically he would not be an employee of NCR. He could keep his AT&T severance and beat the system.

The manager could make all the necessary arrangements. Was he game? "Let me think about it," Kyle replied. *No reason to appear overeager*, he said to himself, even as he privately exulted: *A real job!*

By this time, though, Kyle had been talking on and off for several years with an old friend and coworker who was eager to start up a business. He thought Kyle might serve as his partner and East Coast sales representative.

The firm would sell customized software designed for the sales departments of small and medium-sized companies. The product had definite potential, Kyle believed, but the plan still had the obvious risk of any start-up venture. Almost all of Kyle's compensation would be contingent on making the requisite deals.

After a decade and a half as a company man, part of Kyle thrilled at the prospect of recreating himself as an independent entrepreneur. But his childhood friend Ernest, now a very successful salesman, gently cautioned him. Abandoning his corporate identity was long overdue, Ernest agreed, but could Kyle really transform himself into an intrepid salesman? "Kyle," Ernest told him, "when you work in sales, you've got to be a closer."

Jan, too, was dubious. "Becoming an entrepreneur has always been a fantasy for Kyle, and in some ways he has the personality to be a salesman. He puts people at ease, and he's quietly persuasive. But does he have the drive to be out on his own? If he had that in him, would he have stayed with AT&T for fourteen years?"

Kyle decided to keep both options open. Since his friend thought it would probably be another year before the venture would seriously begin, he could pursue the consulting work and make contacts related to the start-up in his spare time. At some point, though, Kyle would have to make a full-time commitment to the business or walk away.

He accepted NCR's proposition to join the payroll of the consulting firm and work full-time on NCR assignments. (In what seems a fitting illustration of the impersonality of his new workplace, Kyle became an employee of the consulting firm without ever meeting anyone there. He spoke with one of the owners on the phone, then received the necessary paperwork by fax.) In a further irony, Kyle was assigned to work on a multi-year consulting project for AT&T. As a result, he began to spend several days a week in a suite of offices in AT&T's headquarters in Basking Ridge, New Jersey.

After a few months of this arrangement, Kyle began to see himself as an example of the metaphor made famous by British management theorist Charles Handy, who has likened the emerging workplace to a shamrock leaf: a small core of full-time employees perform the essential tasks of the organization, while a contingent staff on a separate leaf take care of less critical work. Then Kyle's superiors at NCR let it be known that they would like Kyle to become a regular full-time employee of NCR. They wanted to bring him into the core.

What's in it for me? Kyle asked himself—a question he had never posed during his years at AT&T. "I don't necessarily want to be an employee of a company anymore. But then again, what are my options?" For a while he could continue to work for NCR as a consultant. But by the end of the year, Kyle predicted, his boss at NCR would say to him, "Come work for us or we'll cut you loose."

Still, he now had considerable leverage in negotiating a deal. After just a few months, he had become a respected team leader on the company project. As Kyle had expected, his inside knowledge of the secrets and soft spots of the AT&T bureaucracy had proved valuable.

He calculated that he could extend his tenure as a consultant, and then demand more money if and when he became a regular employee.

That, in the end, is what happened.

"I'm with AT&T for 14 years and I'm downsized. I am then picked up by consultants who have a contract to work for NCR, a former division of AT&T, which has a contract to work for . . . AT&T. And by the way, I'm making more money." This was the amusing version of the story he told at dinner parties. More seriously, when Kyle looks back at the winding path that led him to his current state, he says, "There can be no retreat to the old dependence that I once felt as a company man at AT&T."

The coincidence of losing his father and his AT&T career on the same day seems potently symbolic to Kyle. "Was I saying goodbye to my real father *and* my pseudo-father?" he asks himself.

As that false farewell letter from Bob Allen will always remind him, AT&T is nobody's family.

8   FATHER AND SON: SOLITARY RETREAT

Tom Chase

My fiftieth year had come and gone,
I sat, a solitary man . . .

Things said or done long years ago,
Or things I did not do or say
But thought that I might say or do,
Weigh me down, and not a day
But something is recalled,
My conscience or my vanity appalled.

—W. B. Yeats, "Vacillation"

We end as we began, with a story of father and son. Yet some life histories ultimately belong in no definable category; they only reveal the particular truths of one human experience. This is the story of Tom Chase.

Mid-morning, early May. The sun is not strong, and a gentle breeze masks a slight chill. Thomas Chase sits at a wooden picnic table outside his 220-year-old stone house, which has been on the market for the better part of a year. Taking in the scent of freshly-cut grass, Tom gazes at a hill in the distance. One afternoon not long ago he spied a flock of beautiful blue herons as they spiraled, crested the hill, and flew away.

He is tall and wiry, with the strong, deep voice of a man who has always loved to sing hymns. His blue eyes are limpid and sad, his teeth stained from countless unfiltered Camels. Tom has a ruddy, weathered face—the face of a handsome fifty-one-year-old man who finds himself adrift and alone.

"This will be my last spring here," Tom says. "Nineteen ninety-six will be my last spring with my girls."

Tom was laid off from his job as a middle manager at AT&T in the summer of 1994, when his nine-man division was eliminated as part of a companywide downsizing. He found a brief stint of part-time consulting and a few months of full-time work, but otherwise Tom has been unemployed for more than two years.

His marriage has not survived the strain. Soon his two daughters— Abigail, twelve, and Amity, nine—will move from their home in Hackettstown, New Jersey, to join their mother, who took a new job and moved to New Hampshire.

"It's getting close to the time," Tom says. "It's sinking in. Am I coming to terms with it? I suppose I am. It's not like I can wave my magic wand. I haven't seen the fairy godmother lately.

"My daughter Amity broke down the other night. When it gets the best of her, she says, 'Daddy, it's just too hard.' And it is. It breaks my heart." He is a private man, but the ache overwhelms him, and his eyes fill with tears.

A graduate of Deerfield and Harvard, a Vietnam veteran and former VISTA volunteer, Tom is exceptionally bright and articulate, with an engaging mind and a good heart. His life has held great promise, which has never been fulfilled.

His story is full of complication and contradiction. It is the confluence of an unusual and powerful family, the forces of history—polio, Vietnam, 1950s prosperity, and 1990s downsizing—and all the untouchable mysteries that come together to make a life. As these influences have coalesced in Tom, they have produced a chronic, painful paralysis.

He has made many self-defeating choices, exacerbated by a kind of stubborn passivity and manifested most starkly in more than three decades of drink before Tom finally confronted his addiction at the age of forty-nine. Says Tom's older sister Alison, with great empathy and an abiding love, "It is a shapeless life."

A kind man and a good father, Tom confounds the people who care about him. "He has gone through life pocket-vetoing his own potential. It's a little like the story of the prodigal son," says his disappointed father. Howard Chase is eighty-seven and he speaks, he says, "in grief and guilt."

Integrating work and identity is difficult for anyone, but it is an essential life journey. Tom never quite took the first step. He drifted with the wind, stifling any voices he did not want to hear.

In 1979 AT&T symbolized the stability and security that Tom had shunned for so much of his life. When he took a job there at the age of thirty-three, it appeared that he had taken control of his life—or at least placed himself on a safe track. But Tom was too creative, too independent, and far too mistrustful of authority to ever flourish as a company man. Though he made several substantial contributions during his tenure at AT&T, and found satisfaction in some of the work, the corporation was never his world. Yet he stayed there for fifteen years.

"The AT&T downsizing was not a causal factor of anything. It was just one incident, a predictable incident," Tom's father says sadly. But the layoff proved a critical catalyst that left Tom completely immobilized. The theme of his story is not so strange, Tom says with a dry laugh: "Privileged, intelligent man loses his bearings."

The Chases were a charmed clan—attractive, intelligent, and accomplished. Howard was a smart, ambitious University of Iowa graduate who became a prominent public relations executive, the assistant secretary of commerce under Truman, and an official in Eisenhower's 1952 campaign. His wife, Betty (who died in 1992), was a slim, beautiful Wellesley graduate—very sharp, a little vain. She was a *Time* magazine researcher who went on to run a successful consulting firm until she gave it up and moved to suburbia.

The Chases believed in intellectual achievement and tangible, public performance. The moral compass was strong and unwavering. Emotions were restrained.

The family lived in the kind of upper-middle-class comfort that blanketed certain American suburbs of the 1950s and 1960s. Ho-Ho-Kus, in northwestern New Jersey, was on the outer edge of suburbia in those years, near lush, rolling country. The Chase house was rambling and graciously decorated—lovely antiques, comfortable furniture and, always, fresh flowers from the garden. The main house had fifteen rooms, six fireplaces, and countless nooks and crannies and secret hiding places. On the six-acre property there was also a carriage house and a wonderful big red barn. The children ran freely through the property, which felt like its own little world.

Their father was mostly absent while the children were growing up. Howard led the peripatetic existence of an American corporate executive of the 1950s and 1960s; invariably, his work came first. Betty threw her considerable energy and intelligence into volunteer work and became an important force in the community. But she was often restless and unhappy, vaguely disappointed in herself for sacrificing her own career to accommodate her family.

There was money for prep schools and European vacations, servants and housekeepers. Every night at seven o'clock, dinner was served by a cook in a formal dining room. On an old wooden stand was a Webster's unabridged dictionary, frequently consulted in family debates. Conversation was a competitive sport. "You could say nothing, but if you did speak, you had better be prepared," Tom recalls.

All three children were tall, good-looking, and verbally precocious. Tom's two older sisters—Anne, born in 1938, and Alison, born in 1942 (three years before Tom)—were cheerful overachievers. This had the predictable effect of pleasing their parents and intimidating their younger brother. Expectations were more often implicit than explicit, but all three children knew that success and accomplishment were very important to their mother and father. (Anne went on to receive her B.A. from Columbia University; Alison graduated from Wellesley.)

"Failure was not condoned in any way," Anne says. "It was simply not in the vocabulary."

Both of Tom's sisters are bright and attractive, with the beautiful blue eyes that are the family signature. Anne has an open face and a direct, no-nonsense manner. Alison looks like someone who roots for the underdog, which she does; her smile is gentle.

Like Tom, they have waged their own private battles. They each divorced, remarried, and confronted difficult personal crises at different points in their lives. In 1983, in the very early days of white-collar downsizing, Anne was a senior marketing executive at Lea and Perrins when her position was eliminated during a restructuring. She regrouped and works today as a consultant, telecommuting from her home office in the White Mountains of New Hampshire. Alison was a single mother in 1982 with two young children to support when she launched her career teaching English at a New Jersey community college.

Both women eventually created lives that were successful in their own terms. From an early age, Tom traveled a different path. Was that a choice? Tom himself, when he feels the weight of his father's Presbyterianism, might say that he met a different fate.

―――――――――

Tom was nine years old—a skinny, athletic third grader—when he was stricken with polio in 1954. The second and fourth graders in his school were all given the new Salk vaccine; the third grade was the control group. Strange misfortunes have struck Tom throughout his life, but none of them more haunting than this—getting one of the last cases of polio because he was given an empty placebo.

The family was in the middle of dinner one October evening when Tom rose from the table. "I don't feel well," he said, his voice already weak. "May I be excused?"

Tom put himself to bed. When he awoke in the middle of the night, he could not move. He let out a horrifying scream, and his mother raced to his room.

Minutes later, the family's housekeeper swept Tom up in her arms and carried him outside in the middle of a terrible storm. As the wind howled, she placed Tom in an ambulance and he was taken to Bergen Pines, the local hospital that treated most of the area's polio victims. His father, away on business as he so often was, flew home at once. That night Tom's fever spiked to 107 degrees, and for the next two days he floated near death.

The doctors kept Tom in isolation for two weeks. Only his parents and a preacher were allowed to see him. "I don't know how the preacher got into the act. Apparently they aren't supposed to carry germs," Howard recalls. "The picture stays with me, of Tom in this caged bed, in a totally blank, white room. He was in prison." His parents stood frozen in their vigil, waiting to see if their son would be spared. Tom remembers a painful spinal tap; forty years later, the memory alone makes him wince.

When he was let out of isolation, he shared a room with a two-year-old boy named Ernie. Terrified but unable to turn away, Tom stared at him all day long. "Every morning I would see that Ernie's leg had become more and more deformed, until one morning he was crippled."

When a hurricane blew out the hospital's electricity, Tom was alone in his room. Medical equipment crashed around him as the nurses scrambled to keep the power on for patients on iron lungs.

After he left the hospital, the doctors kept Tom out of school for three months and denied him any physical activity for six months. Tom was lucky; he suffered no permanent paralysis. But his recovery was sluggish and fitful, as any progress in his life was fated to be.

Tom's weight had fallen from one hundred pounds to sixty. To rebuild his strength, his mother took him outside and walked with him every day along the path that separated the main house and the carriage house.

"Before I went into the hospital," Tom recalls with a rueful smile, "Chuckie Thompson and I were the fastest runners our age. Afterward, I never could run as fast. Never did whup Chuckie Thompson again in Memorial Day foot races."

"I never considered the polio a major life incident, just a pain in the ass," Tom says, instinctively drawing upon the bravado that is his characteristic armor. His sisters' perspective must be closer to the mark. "The polio was a critical fact of his life," Alison says. "The psychological impact had to be significant," Anne agrees.

When a person is not physically disfigured by the disease, he may emotionally cripple himself. This was a common observation of polio victims in the years before the Salk vaccine, and for Tom it seems to hold more than a grain of truth.

The illness intensified a family dynamic that was already entrenched. As the youngest child and the only boy, Tom was indulged by his mother and particularly by Nellie, a family housekeeper. Affectionate, wonderfully intuitive, given to expansive hugs and sweet laughter, Nellie was in many ways the nurturing figure in the household (the children called her Nana), and she absolutely adored Tom. Tom would remain similarly devoted to Nellie, who never quite left the family's orbit until she died in 1994.

During the recuperation, Tom's illness dominated the family, and the indulgence was unlimited. "We were not to pick on him, we were not to cross him; he got what he wanted. *Spoiled* would be the old-fashioned word," says Alison. A family pattern had been established, Alison suggests: Other people take care of Tom and, consequently, Tom never quite learns how to take care of himself.

Before polio struck, Tom had already found the great friendship of his youth. Johnny Costanza, his classmate and neighbor, was a fellow polio victim; unlike Tom, Johnny would wear braces on both legs for the rest of his life. Short, chunky, with massive shoulders and an infectious smile, Johnny was an offbeat character and a spirited survivor. From the age of six, the two boys were inseparable.

Tom's father did not think much about it at the time, but looking back, he sees their alliance as a conspiracy: "It was Tom and Johnny against the world, Tom and Johnny against an orderly society. There was a flamboyance to their antics. There was a rail on a bridge nearby, above a river, and the boys would walk the rail. That was courage, but it was stupid courage."

Tom's father still cannot grasp the essential goodness, the innocence and intensity of this classic preadolescent friendship. But that, too, seems of a piece with a larger pattern—of a father and son who have loved each other but circled round each other, never quite sharing the same space.

As Tom's friendship with Johnny deepened, their escapades grew more destructive. By the time they were adolescents, and before anyone realized what had happened, Tom and Johnny had become serious drinkers.

One night, not long after Tom turned twelve, Alison and her mother arrived home to find him blindly drunk on the front porch. Tom and Johnny had been drinking, and somehow Tom managed to ride home on his bicycle. Because Tom's mother was totally distraught, his sister got him into bed and nursed him through a severe toxic reaction, spoon-feeding him sips of water as she sat and held his hand.

The two boys seemed destined to remain close friends, but once again Tom's life was touched by tragedy. Johnny was killed in a car crash a few weeks after he turned twenty-one. He had just gotten engaged, and had seemed so happy when he made plans to celebrate Tom's own birthday later that month.

At the accident scene, Tom stared at a huge pothole in a curve of the road. Johnny was probably drunk, and certainly driving too fast, when his car hit the pothole, swerved off the road and slammed into a wall.

Tom was a pallbearer at Johnny's funeral. He sees it, still, as the saddest day of his life.

When he was fourteen, Tom attended Alison's graduation from the Dwight School, a private girls' school in the area. "She was the president of everything, the recipient of countless awards," her father recalls with paternal pride. Tom sat silently in the audience. Afterward, he walked up to his sister. "Sis," he said in a small voice. "What's left for me?"

Alison heard a child's cry for help. "He was in despair," she says. Tom's question would resonate through the years. It became an emblematic family story, told slightly differently by each member of the clan. Howard's version is inevitably more judgmental. To him, "Tom had spoken as though he were casting a vote on his own future."

That year, Tom was packed off to boarding school as he entered the ninth grade. "I wasn't browbeaten into going," Tom says. "You appear to have a choice, but you don't really. One of those deals." But his days at Deerfield would be among the happiest of his life.

His father had wanted him to go to St. Paul's, a more conventionally prestigious school that was eager to have him. But when Tom visited Deerfield, Frank Boyden, the school's celebrated headmaster, asked to see him. They sat in the headmaster's study by a bay window that overlooked the playing fields. Boyden pointed out to Tom, a young history buff, where the Indians had come up over the ridge during the battle of Deerfield in 1704.

"I see that young fellow has hooked up a sleigh. Would you like to go for a ride?" the headmaster asked. Tom was enraptured. He would become one of the protégés of Boyden and his wife (who were immortalized by John McPhee in his biography, *The Headmaster*). Tom loved the old-fashioned New England academy, its academic rigor and its Sunday night sings. He played baseball and earned grades that were good enough for him to be accepted into Harvard. "Good memories," Tom says, "fond memories."

It still pains Tom to recall his father's disapproval of his prep school years, which Howard expressed when he first saw Tom's senior yearbook and repeats again from a distance of three decades. "It says a lot about Tom," Howard comments. "There was just one line under his picture. Baseball squad. No music, no debate, no clubs, nothing."

The story is as old as the species—the powerful father and his melancholy son.

Howard Chase is a man of the world who believes that opportunities should be seized: "A man should leave footprints in the snow." Success should be earned and unambiguous, as it was for Howard his entire working life.

Wordlessly, Tom refused the example that had been set before him. In the face of his father's staggering drive, Tom cut himself loose. His only motion was flight.

When Tom arrived at Harvard in the fall of 1963, he had already started to run. After three semesters of drinking and failing grades, he was asked to take a year's leave. He signed on with VISTA (Volunteers In Service To America, a federal agency), which had only just been established in 1964. Tom was in the second training class for volunteers.

In Minnesota he worked with the Cloquet Band of Chippewa Indians, where he made use of his own antipathy for bureaucracy by giving a course in how to deal with the Bureau of Indian Affairs. "This was the most backward organization around," Tom recalls. "There would be federal grant money available for indoor plumbing, say, but a tribe member would get some civil servant at the bureau who would demand everything in quintuplicate, and he'd just give up." Tom showed them how to fight back.

By then it was the summer of 1966. Since Tom had only a probationary status at Harvard, his student deferment was about to expire, right in the middle of the Vietnam war. Feeling like he had nothing better to do, he enlisted in the army. After eight weeks of basic training at Fort Dix, Tom was sent to intelligence school at Fort Holabird, Maryland. He did very well on the mandated battery of tests and for a brief interlude it seemed that he might get lucky. He was about to be sent to language school in California (to learn Czech) when he received a telegram: Orders revoked. Tom was to report to Fort Bragg, where he would be trained for Special Forces—the Green Berets. "I didn't have any great desire to go to Vietnam," Tom says. At the time, of course, he must have known it would not be easy to avoid that journey.

Before he went overseas, at the age of twenty-one, Tom married

Holly, his childhood sweetheart. They had known each other since they were in kindergarten, and Tom had stayed smitten. Perhaps Tom felt a need to marry quickly; his friend Johnny had been engaged to be married when he died just a few months before. His sister, Anne, has always wondered if there was a connection between the two events. Certainly Tom's parents made it clear that they thought their son was too young to marry—defying them in this choice, at least, felt good.

———————

Tom arrived in Vietnam as a roving intelligence operative based in Bin Hoa, north of Saigon. He got a close view of the mindless bureaucracy of the military, and he also saw a fair amount of combat. "The worst thing is to be under artillery fire," Tom says. "Tet was the scariest. Three and a half, four hours, the most frightening of my life. We were crouched under a tin shack with sandbags on top that wouldn't stop a bullet from a rifle."

Terror was random and pervasive. "Crispy Critters was a game we played," Tom recalls. "You'd set rats on fire and see how far they would run. Our whole camp almost got killed one night when a rat nearly fell on a magazine of four-and-a-half-inch mortar rounds."

Tom's father had mixed feelings about his son's decision to enlist. But when he had an unexpected chance to visit Tom in Vietnam, it had the effect of bringing the two men truly together for the first time.

In 1968, Howard was working as a PR man when he took an assignment to work as a registered spokesman for the South Korean government. He would be part of a five-man mission to advise the Seoul government on economic policy. A few weeks before he was to leave for Southeast Asia, Howard attended a meeting of the Council on Foreign Relations in New York. There he met General Westmoreland, commander of U.S. forces in Vietnam.

"My son's in Vietnam," he told the general.

"Where is he?" Westmoreland asked.

"I'm sorry I can't tell you, General," Howard replied. "That's classified information."

Westmoreland roared. "Well, if you ever find yourself in Vietnam, tell anyone that you have an invitation to come see me. We'll find your son."

When he left for Seoul, Howard took with him a letter of introduction that President Eisenhower had written to the President of South Korea. When Howard presented it at the Blue House (the Korean White House), to his surprise they named him an honorary colonel in the Dove division of their army—one of the two fighting divisions sent to Vietnam.

And so Howard found himself one Sunday morning on a Cathay Airlines flight from Seoul to Saigon; the government had arranged for him to tour a number of the Korean camps in Vietnam. Given the circumstances, Howard thought he might as well take General Westmoreland up on his offer. Soon after his plane touched down, he was driven to Westmoreland's office.

"It was 11:00 A.M." Howard remembers. "Westmoreland said, Come back at two o'clock and be prepared to go someplace. So I came back and was immediately given a camouflage suit. They directed me to an army Caribou airplane that was delivering—literally—one cow, six pigs, and one hundred ducks. We headed to a camp about forty miles from the Cambodian border.

"Tom didn't know I was within twelve thousand miles of him. I was told that we'd have one hour together. I saw Tom holding a .30-caliber machine gun. He didn't seem to hear me as I approached. When I tapped him on his shoulder, his mouth fell open and his eyes practically fell out of his head. He put both hands on my shoulders and said, 'My God, Pop, we must be losing the war!'"

Tom was granted a leave, and for the next ten days he traveled with his father. It was just the two of them and a Korean general in a helicopter, sweeping into jungles and hillsides to inspect Korean military camps.

One day Tom and his father watched the South Koreans occupy a village. Everyone was summoned from their huts. A Korean captain then explained, in fluent Vietnamese, that in return for Korean protection, it was incumbent upon the villagers to let them know if they saw any Viet Cong lurking about.

"These were six-foot bruisers, the elite of the South Korean army," Tom says. "For light entertainment the Korean sergeant who was a champion at tae kwan do [a kind of karate] would do something like chop down a tree with his bare hand." The villagers took the hint.

By this time, Tom's views had shifted; he was disgusted with both the military prosecution of the war and the American press in roughly equal measure. Working in intelligence, Tom and his colleagues would frequently advise senior officers that Viet Cong were coming down a certain route at a certain time, and that the ARVN (Army of the Republic of Vietnam) should be prepared for them. Instead, the ARVN troops would be moved, a few miles east or west, just to get out of the way. "That really curdled Tom," his father remembers.

"I guess I believe that a lesson of Vietnam is win it or don't fight it," Tom says. "We cut and ran. I don't know what the honorable way out might have been, but I do know the way we did it was dishonorable."

Just before his father flew back to the States, Tom was promoted to sergeant. "I was asked if I would pin the sergeant's stripes on his sleeve," Howard reports. "So the army may have made him a sergeant, but I put the stripes on his sleeve."

After fourteen months in Vietnam, Tom decided to come home. He has often wondered: what might have happened if he had stayed in the army and made it his career? It was a choice he seriously considered.

"Back in the U.S., I had a certain impulse to stay in the army," Tom says. At this point, his wife was pregnant with their first child, and she would not have encouraged Tom in this choice. But silent parental pressure was probably a stronger deterrent. "One reason I didn't stay is because it would not have met anyone's expectations of what I should be doing," Tom says.

Soon after he returned to the States, Tom declined the opportunity to become a lieutenant. Tom had turned down a similar chance when he was in the middle of basic training. The army desperately needed lieutenants in those days, because so many of them had been killed. As a result, Tom says, "they were really scraping the bottom of the barrel." This was the generation, he adds, of William Calley, the infamous lieutenant who led the My Lai massacre.

When Howard looks back on Tom's decision to reject the army's second offer to make him a lieutenant, he sees it as "a failure to seize what other people would see as an advantage, an opportunity for self-improvement. That has always meant very little to Tom."

That is a revisionist reading of history, Tom says with a half-smile. "Another missed opportunity? Sure. But this was not a choice that would have made anyone happy at the time."

When Tom came home in April 1968 he saw himself as a lucky survivor, a whole man while so many others were maimed and crippled. It was an uncanny echo of his bout with polio. From both disasters he walked away physically unscathed—but the invisible scars are inevitably more difficult to discern.

For Tom, the subject has always been sensitive: "You can say what happened. You cannot say how it made you feel." When he returned from Vietnam, he did not talk much about his experiences, even as he suffered post-traumatic stress. At one point, living in a house where the noise of passing trucks could sound like gunfire, Tom would sometimes wake up and find that he had slept under the bed.

United with his wife and infant daughter, Tom reenrolled in college—and for a second time, he walked into Harvard Yard with no particular sense of purpose. The legacy of the war was still very fresh, and Tom had no clear notion of what his future might hold. Once again, he chose the path of least resistance.

Harvard's entire undergraduate student body that year included just ten Vietnam veterans. One of them, a young man named Dick Wachs, became a good friend of Tom's. As a sergeant in Special Forces, Dick had won a Silver Star, the second-highest award for gallantry. One morning they were both walking toward the registrar's office when they saw that the building was blockaded in a protest against the Cambodian invasion. "We thought about this awhile," Tom says, "and then we drove home, changed into our full Green Beanie suits, minus any weapons, and drove back to Harvard Yard. As we walked toward the registrar's office, you'd have thought it was the Red Sea. We saw a lot of unpleasant expressions, but no one said a word."

Like many veterans, Tom was appalled by the antiwar movement. His politics, which were always conservative, became staunchly right-wing. One classroom exchange evokes the strain that Tom felt during these days. "The course was called Nat Sci 9. This was a highly politicized astronomy class," Tom says with a laugh. "Anyway, some kid in the class, a gorgeous boy with this cherubic face, starts in about My Lai. "I don't know what got into me. I said to him, 'I've seen whole villages wiped out, the women raped, the old people killed and the young men taken as slaves. I saw one village with 650 bodies. And *they* did it, the Viet Cong.'

"So this kid turns to me and says, 'You saw that?'

"I said, 'Yes, I did.'

"He said, 'Your experience is irrelevant.' Quote, unquote.

"I'll never forget it. 'Your experience is irrelevant.'"

Tom's parents had loaned him money to buy a small house in Arlington, Massachusetts—an American flag flew on the porch—and Tom and his wife lived there until Tom finished his degree. His eldest daughter, Jessica, was born in 1969, and Victoria (known as Tory) was born three years later.

After Tom graduated in 1972, the family moved to North Carolina, where Tom worked as a mortgage banker. But Tom was drinking heavily by this time, and under that weight his marriage collapsed. Within two years, Tom suffered a double loss: his wife left him, taking their two daughters with her, and the firm that he worked for went bankrupt.

In many ways, the next chapter of Tom's life foreshadowed the more dire fallout from the AT&T layoff. It was a desultory interlude, and it lasted for more than four years.

He could not move.

The sudden loss of his family and his job left him powerless, unable to take any action at all. Whether one calls this innate passivity or clinical depression or simply a basic failure of will, in Tom it goes very deep. He feels its pull even as he knows the damage it has done, to himself and to all the people who love him. Typically, Tom speaks of it bluntly, quickly, and with an endearing shrug. "Most of my shortcomings," he says, "come from an impulse to say, 'To hell with it.'"

Tom's mother, Betty, understood this quality in her only son, and it troubled her. In a letter to her daughter Alison, written just after Tom's first marriage broke up, she wrote:

> He was suffering intensely, as you knew he would be, about his broken marriage and most particularly about his separation from his beloved little daughters. He loves them dearly and is a remarkably good father. ... He has great intelligence and (at least in my opinion) considerable charm. I am sure that he will find a good job and be able to reconstitute his life. Certainly his first twenty-nine years have been filled with blows, most of which seem undeserved.

Tom and his mother had a publicly stormy relationship, punctuated by bitter arguments—usually about politics—that began in Tom's adolescence and continued throughout his adulthood. But the strain between them was superficial; in the midst of battle, their anger would suddenly dissipate. During one notorious family dinner, Tom recalls, "My mother called me a damn fascist and I called her a pinko fellow traveler, but then we just stopped and talked about gardening."

Fundamentally, they liked each other as much as they loved each other. Tom and his mother shared an easy affection and found many of the same pleasures in life. Betty, like her husband, set high standards for her son, but she also understood why Tom did not or could not meet them. At his mother's funeral, Tom eloquently described her legacy:

> What she taught me, in no particular order:
> How to make amaryllis bloom year after year.
> How to skip for a first-grade play.
> An abiding curiosity. . . .
> How to keep a jade plant alive for twenty-five years.
> And finally, she taught me that the unreserved love of a mother for an

often undeserving son is one of the strongest forces in the universe—and if I ever become the person I should be, I will owe it to the love and faith she gave me and gives me still, I think."

Those undeserved blows that Tom's mother had noted had already taken their toll. Here was Tom, at the age of twenty-nine, an unemployed mortgage banker in the depths of the most severe real estate recession the nation had seen since the 1930s. Tom moved from North Carolina to Cos Cobb, Connecticut (his parents then lived in Stamford), and he lived for a time on a boat. Working as a fix-it-man in a machine shop, he repaired small engines on lawnmowers and chainsaws.

Then Tom met a beautiful girl, and suddenly he was full of hope. She was tall and blonde, with an earthy quality that Tom found enticing. They embarked on a passionate, tumultuous affair that ended when she left Tom. Her rejection was devastating to Tom, more painful even than the breakup of his marriage.

During this period, Tom's parents watched their son floundering—unable or unwilling, as they saw it, to choose his life's work. Had he been left alone at this critical moment, Tom might have made a choice of his own. But his father could not bear to see him squandering his intelligence, talent, and charm; he could not bear to see him *fail*. So he stepped in, and his intervention would prove decisive.

Howard was working as an independent consultant when AT&T asked him to find two people to work in its corporate planning department. A Berkeley Ph.D. was one of the candidates he presented; the other was his own son. "This is nepotism," Howard told the AT&T executive who had recruited him, "but he has all the abilities to do the job. They're just latent." Overnight, he recalls, Tom went from making five dollars an hour to earning $29,000 a year.

"Was it a mistake for Tom to join any large organization?" Howard asks himself years later. "Maybe. Maybe subconsciously we knew that at the time. AT&T was a symbol of security, and Tom had rejected all symbols of security." Howard has spent decades fitfully trying, and consistently failing, to comprehend that rejection.

To meet Howard Chase at the age of eighty-seven is to catch a glimpse of the long shadow he must have cast over his only son. He is a vigorous man, tall, white-haired, and imposing—his considerable intelligence clearly intact. After he was widowed, Howard sold his Stamford home ("Founderville," Tom called it, with his father the founder); he lives today in an expensive semi-retirement apartment house in town. It is a well-appointed four-room apartment: good furniture, artwork from his travels, interesting paintings from the Far East. Scattered about are books and journals, and photos of Howard with his elegant wife through the years. In his office is a good-sized desk and a computer.

Three walls are covered with plaques attesting to Howard's accomplishments, along with photos of him with Presidents Eisenhower and Johnson. He is proud of his past, and with good reason.

The son of a farm implement dealer, Howard grew up in a middle-class family in Sioux City, Iowa. "I graduated with the highest honors in my class from the University of Iowa. Then I went to the London School of Economics for a year. After working at the University of Iowa as a housing director, I made my way to Harvard. Nobody there had heard of me, but I introduced myself to the graduate dean, and within fifteen minutes I was admitted without any credentials. A year later I was named an assistant instructor in international relations."

Howard met Betty Coykendall on a blind date in Ames, Iowa, in the summer of 1932, when Betty was eighteen and he was twenty-two. In the fall of 1935, while Betty was a senior at Wellesley, they married in secret, since it was grounds for expulsion at the women's college. ("They'll strip off all my buttons if they ever find out," Betty told Howard at the time.)

Howard worked as an editorial writer at the *Des Moines Register* for several years before he decided to try his hand at public relations. After a stint as a vice president of the American Retail Foundation in Washington, Howard became the first director of public relations at the General Mills Corporation at the age of thirty-one.

Howard tells the tale with characteristic gusto—he has always told a good story—and its theme is unmistakable: he was an ambitious young man, and his ambitions were amply and justly rewarded. A Washington acquaintance, it seems, had passed his name along to an executive at General Mills.

"I had lunch in the Brook Club in New York with James Ford Bell, the chairman of General Mills," Howard recalls. "*Time* magazine had just called him chipmunk-jowled, and he was a bit annoyed about that.

"After a while he offered me a job. I had been making $9,000 a year at that point, and he offered me $15,000. I said I regretted it, the challenge would be wonderful, but I couldn't possibly take the job for less than $18,000.

"Bell told me, 'I'm inclined to grant that, but with a codicil. You'll be more harshly judged at eighteen [thousand] than you would be at fifteen.'"

"That took me aback," Howard laughs, "but I told him that was a risk I was prepared to take."

He was on his way to Minneapolis when the Japanese bombed Pearl Harbor. Howard wanted to take some part in the war effort, and his new employer granted him a leave to become an administrative assistant in the War Food Administration.

He went on to have a brief but interesting political career. In 1947, Howard was named assistant secretary of commerce in the Truman administration. Nearly five years later, he got a close look at General Eisenhower on the eve of his decision to run for president for the first time.

In late 1951, Eisenhower's supporters were drafting a group of politicians, businessmen, and celebrities to try to persuade the General to run for president. One of them was Howard Chase. In November he received a phone call from Paul Hoffman, the former administrator of the Marshall Plan and a close associate of Eisenhower's, inviting him to lunch. Henry Cabot Lodge would join them. The meal had barely begun when Hoffman posed the obviously rhetorical question: Would Howard be willing to go to Paris, where Eisenhower was stationed as the supreme allied commander of NATO, and speak to one of the greatest military commanders in history?

"Before I left," Howard recalls, "I went to talk to Herbert Hoover, who was living in the Waldorf Hotel at the time. Hoover advised against an Eisenhower candidacy, for two reasons. First, he said, Eisenhower didn't have the 'fighting space'—those were his words—to run a domestic political campaign. Then he went on to say that he had it on good authority that the Democrats were compiling a book on Eisenhower's alleged sexual peccadilloes."

From Monday to Friday, Howard lived in Eisenhower's magnificent mansion outside Paris. "I'd go with him to his office, sit in a deep green chair with my feet tucked under me, and watch the world's great traipse in and out. I kept silent.

"On Friday, he had reserved the whole morning for me. 'Let's get to work,' he said. So I told him how I had gotten there and what Hoover had said about 'fighting space' and sex.

"'Let's take these one at a time,' Eisenhower said. He was sort of talking to himself, scraping his legs with a swagger stick. Then he told me his life history in terms of women. He had a great awe of women, I thought.

"On the question of 'fighting space,' he went to a wall and pulled down a series of maps, and proceeded to describe theories of sea power.

"Then he asked me, 'Is there anything else?'

"I said, 'no sir.'

"He thought for a moment. And then he said, 'Well, if this is what I have to take, I'll do it.'"

This conversation was some three months before the evening in February 1952 when, as historian Stephen Ambrose tells the story, the famous aviator Jacqueline Cochran led the final push to persuade Eisenhower to run. Cochran had flown to Paris to play for the general a two-hour film of a rally in Madison Square Garden in which about fifteen thousand people were gathered, chanting, "We want Ike."

Eisenhower was deeply moved by the film, and when Cochran offered an impulsive toast ("To the President . . ."), he burst into tears. "Cochran's dramatic presentation," Ambrose writes, "convinced him that the people wanted him." Not long after, he told Clay and other close associates that he would indeed run.

Howard faced reversals later in his life, most notably when his public-relations firm started losing money and he was forced to shut it down. Middle-aged and out of work, he had some anxious moments, but they were willfully ignored. From adversity comes strength: that is Howard's credo, and he has lived it.

"I wrote a four-line letter to the head of American Can. Two days later I got a phone call inviting me to come up to their Greenwich headquarters, and twenty minutes later I was a vice president. I knew nothing about their business, which was packaging, but the job paid good money. It was a good position, there were cars and drivers."

"He picks himself up, he develops another strategy, he moves on," his daughter Alison says. "He's indomitable."

"It is possible that what appeared to be success bothered Tom," his father says, "or made him doubt his ability to do the same thing. Not that anyone wanted him to do the same thing. . . ." He gazes into the distance. The Chases find no simple answers to these questions.

As a member of the corporate planning staff, Tom became part of AT&T's famous General Departments. Here Tom observed one of the most unyielding bureaucracies of the postwar business world.

The General Departments formed the core of a far-flung organization. As the headquarters staff, it issued directives—which were sometimes obeyed, but often ignored—to the twenty-one operating companies, the local phone systems that later consolidated into the baby Bells.

No one deviated from the protocol. AT&T corporate planners would go out into the field and spend a week or so with the planning department of each local company. (Tom's group included New Jersey Bell, Cincinnati Bell, and Wisconsin Telephone.) They would debate strategies and issues. Then the headquarters planners would return to begin work on the annual data request that went out each year from central headquarters to each of the operating companies—the same guidelines, in other words, were set forth for Illinois Bell and New England Telephone.

The local phone companies were encouraged, but not obliged to follow these missives. They were, however, physically impossible to ignore. "The planning request was literally a three-foot-high stack of binders," Tom recalls.

Tom had been working at AT&T for less than a year when he met Elizabeth, who would become his second wife. "She was the new, wild-haired, attractive twenty-one-year-old girl up in the secretarial pool. I was thirty-three, divorced, looked like an up-and-comer." For months, they were a secret office romance.

Elizabeth's father worked for many years on a GM assembly line. Her formal education ended in high school, but she had a keen intelligence and a powerful ambition. "Elizabeth's background is Irish, Hungarian and Sicilian, okay?" Tom says. "Rambunctious, demonstrative. You have rows, so you don't smolder. I'm a classic WASP—I smolder." They married in 1981.

Once their two daughters were in school, Elizabeth went back to college, graduating from Seton Hall with a 3.9 average. "She's extraordinarily smart, and I was very proud of her success," Tom says. "I got her a little red roadster as a graduation present."

That is only part of the story, of course, as Tom well knows. "She's ambitious," he adds, "and she can't understand why everyone isn't." Inevitably, Tom does not need to add, she found it impossible to understand or accept the absence of ambition in the man she married.

When AT&T sent Tom to Harvard in 1986 for a one-year fellowship, it was an elite assignment. It was also a clear signal that he could shoot up the bureaucratic ladder—if that was what he wanted, and if he obeyed the rules of the race. But Tom never decided what he really wanted, and all too often he flouted corporate convention when it was imperative that he respect it.

While he was at Harvard, the company paid Tom's salary and rent for the year, and Tom and Elizabeth enjoyed their time in Cambridge. But when the time came to write a thesis, Tom indulged his flinty anti-establishment streak. His paper predicted that AT&T's equipment business would be acquired by the German conglomerate Siemens some-time in the 1990s. This was actually quite prophetic: AT&T did sell its equipment business in 1996, albeit to U.S. stockholders rather than a foreign conglomerate. Still, this idea was naturally scorned by the corporate officers who had sent Tom to Harvard in the first place.

Despite his ambivalence toward company life, Tom proved to be a natural corporate strategist. His great talent was his ability to simultaneously see the larger context and also understand the tiniest details of an issue or situation—the essential, and rare, skill of a strategic planner. Chuck Levine, who served for a time as Tom's boss (before he left AT&T to become a senior vice president of Octel and, later, the chief marketing officer at Sprint PCS), admired Tom's intellect: "He has the ability to step back and understand the context of some problem or project. It's the ability to go from the ground level up to fifty thousand feet. He is one of the smartest people I know."

Tom forged an iconoclastic career at AT&T, specializing in strategic planning of one sort or another. His mandate usually was to nudge AT&T to become more creative in the use of its resources, meshing disciplines, processes, and procedures. He rose to the level of district manager, the third of five layers of middle management. Some of his assignments were high profile, and usually they were removed from the rigid confines of the established bureaucracy. Often he worked in "closet" organizations, outside the mainstream. "Some vice president would say, 'We've got to get some out-of-the-box thinking'—the favored phrase at the time—and they would round up the usual suspects to form a small group." Tom was often on the list.

He was first drafted into the so-called Emerging Issues group, which was staffed by just three people. This was a new creation for AT&T and of the three men selected, none were longtime Bell veterans. During this period, most AT&T employees came from one of three "clubs" at the old Ma Bell: Long Lines, the division that ran long-distance service; Western Electric, the equipment manufacturing division; and the operating companies, today's baby Bells. As part of the Emerging Issues group, Tom says, "My job was to coerce or seduce the operating companies into paying more attention to their own territories." Tom and his cohorts were well-suited to the job because they were all "off the street": "I was not from Long Lines, Western Electric, or one of the operating companies. I could talk with any of them, but I was not of them."

In 1979, five years after the Justice Department filed suit to break up AT&T's monopoly, Tom wrote a paper describing what would happen when AT&T lost the suit. This was worse than mischievous; it was terribly rash. The powers that be had no sense of humor about the litigation. "Of course, the paper was quickly tossed," Tom says.

After 1982, when AT&T settled its suit and agreed to the breakup of the Bell System, Tom did strategic planning work in different departments and fiefdoms. "I moved from leader to leader. I got a reputation for being able to find things out and do odd jobs," he says. "Very senior people would call to ask, 'What kind of strategy do the Japanese have?' Or the question would filter down the ranks and some senior vice president would say, 'We desperately need 105 commemorative World War II tank toys.' Could I find some? Well, yes, I could."

The most interesting assignments gave Tom a real intellectual challenge. In the late 1980s, for example, Tom helped launch AT&T's first annual Twenty-First Century Program. In a series of seminars, speeches, and reports, the program tackled the cosmic issues—social, economic, and political—that shape the global environment in which AT&T must compete. Typically, Tom was brought onto the team because a senior executive had to make a keynote speech. An early draft was full of rich material, but it lacked perspective and context. The executive thought Tom was the man to fix it. "They've got this tremendous marble quarry," he told Tom. "I want a cathedral, and they're building me a gas station."

Yet Tom, with his natural creative flair, had no patience with office drudgery—the dreary bureaucratic exercises that every large organization demands. "I am a poor performer of make-work; I just wouldn't do it," Tom says. Adds his former colleague Achmad Hassan, who now works as a business development director for AT&T France: "Because Tom is so exceptionally bright, he wants to do things to the level that he wants. You wouldn't want him for boring, number-crunching stuff. But strategic thinking and insight, that was his strength."

So, too, was Tom's early push for small business. At AT&T in the late 1980s, there was a spirited minority of executives—scattered through the ranks and divisions—who sensed that AT&T was missing the fast-growing small business market. Tom was a charter member of this club, and he helped nudge AT&T to compete better on this turf. "I was carrying the message for small business for years before the company acknowledged its problem in this area."

In 1990, top management deputized Tom to organize an eighteen-week series of seminars focused on the small business customer. Small company owners voiced their complaints with AT&T service, and entrepreneurs spoke to packed auditoriums of employees. The seminars were a great success, a moment of glory for Tom.

During that year, Tom was named a founding member of the Small Business Market team, a nine-man group. This organization was the brainchild of Walter Murphy, who was then an executive vice-president. (Murphy was later killed in the 1996 plane crash that took the lives of U.S. secretary of commerce Ron Brown and the American executives who were traveling with him.)

This very small, self-managed "skunk works" was deliberately positioned outside the corporate bureaucracy. Its mandate was to scour the AT&T empire to discover products or services that could be successfully marketed to small businesses. These autonomous entities would later become commonplace at AT&T, but they were a rarity in the early 1990s.

From the outset, the team faced a basic problem: How does an independent team, beholden to no part of the bureaucracy, persuade that same bureaucracy to act on its recommendations or adopt its ideas? "You could have a corporate sponsor at a high level of the company, a senior vice president or an executive vice president," explains Achmad. "But at the end of the day an idea had to be implemented by a business unit that was part of the bureaucracy." The managers of that unit would get no kudos for coming up with the good idea, but they might be blamed for backing a loser, Achmad explains. "So naturally everyone thinks of a million reasons not to take our suggestions."

Still, Tom's group claimed a few impressive successes. Around 1991, the team proposed the development of a picture phone, which they called the Picasso. (It looks like an ordinary telephone, but once it is plugged in, a video appears on a small screen.) It was first adopted by department store chains, which use it to show new merchandise to their outlets. Later the FDA approved the product for medical use.

The group's position was always precarious. Each year, its funding had to be approved at a senior executive level. For several years, the budget sailed through, but by the spring of 1993 the team was looking increasingly vulnerable. Bureaucratic forces were moving against them, and at the grassroots level there was a changing of the guard that would prove fatal.

Cost cutting had become, once again, a top priority at AT&T. The next round of downsizing, everyone agreed, would likely target more and more small units. Mid-level strategic planners like Tom suddenly seemed a luxury. And even if Tom and his colleagues might have beaten those odds, they could not hope to overcome a new boss, a twenty-six year AT&T veteran named Mike Kenniff.

The team's original boss, Chuck Levine, was widely respected. A former General Electric and Procter & Gamble executive, Levine was an executive director, the highest level of status in the organization below corporate officer. Levine was thought to have a shrewd sense of timing, knowing precisely when to move on. Of such instincts corporate careers are made.

So it was alarming one morning when Levine announced that he would be leaving the team. He would be looking around for his replacement, he told his troops.

Soon the troops began to look around, too. "On our floor we noticed this fellow Mike Kenniff," one of Tom's coworkers recalls. "He was between assignments, and we knew that he spent a lot of time talking to Chuck." Earlier, Kenniff has been interviewed by the team to see if he might make a good fit with the group; that was part of the collegial, democratic spirit of the project. Suddenly, though, Levine was walking by, introducing Kenniff as the team's new boss.

"We could see the handwriting on the wall," says Tom's former colleague. "We knew this would be the downfall of our group." Kenniff was only a division manager, the fourth level of the management hierarchy, while Levine had been an executive director, the elite form of fifth-level manager. There is a vast distance between these rungs on the ladder: directors receive stock options, free financial advice, and other assorted perks. To move from one level to the next is to make a major leap in status. If their new boss was anything less than a director, the team feared, they would not gain the necessary access to senior management. And without that support, their mission had no future.

In the oblique way that companies often signal their secret plans, AT&T let Tom and his cohorts know that their jobs were in jeopardy. The group's modest request to make a prototype of a new kind of cellular phone was turned down, with no plausible explanation; a few months earlier, it would have been routinely approved. "When that proposal was denied," Tom says, "I knew things looked bad."

Then there came the familiar rumble—layoffs were coming, and soon. It was the fall of 1993, possibly January 1994, recalls one of the team members, when he confronted Kenniff and asked the obvious question: "Will there be involuntary layoffs?"

"Don't worry," Kenniff replied.

Several months later, in June 1994, the small business team was summoned to an empty conference room. The group was being eliminated as part of a downsizing drive; layoffs would be involuntary. The team members must abide by the usual procedures. Everyone was "at risk," and so they had sixty days to find a new job within the company. If they failed, they were fired.

"They brought in a real nice lady from personnel," Tom recalls. "Her job was to turn out the lights when everyone was gone." The moment they were declared to be at risk, Tom and his teammates suddenly had no work to do. That was perhaps the strangest feeling of all.

During the course of this year—between Kenniff's arrival in the spring of 1993 and the demise of the group in June 1994—Tom escaped, more and more, to a bottle of bourbon. He would miss meetings, and his memos would not get written. His colleagues could not be sure that he would do what he said he'd do.

"When the frustration set in," Tom says, "when it was clear that our team was going to be run into the ground, what happened to me was rather than fight it, I said, 'to hell with it.'" This is the sadly familiar re-frain of his life, spoken now with a more potent force.

As it happened, Tom's new boss, Mike Kenniff, seemed to be tar-geting Tom as soon as he arrived on the scene. A member of the team recalls one particular encounter: "There was a group meeting in which Tom presented a very interesting idea based on some new chip that he had found at Bell Labs. Kenniff just jumped all over him. 'Oh, this will never work.' He just dismissed it out of hand. He went after Tom with a vengeance."

When he looks back upon his career at AT&T, Tom feels bitter about the management debacles that necessitated the downsizing of his small division. He is angrier at himself for staying much too long in a place he never belonged. Yet he can still acknowledge that he saw something good, even noble, in AT&T in his early years. He witnessed the waning days of a corporate culture that inspired many employees, including himself, to believe in the company's mandate.

"Everybody should have a telephone, universal service—that was a worthy mission. It was good work. Sure, there was an arrogance to it: 'We'll serve you our way, but by God, we'll serve you. And your tele-phone is going to work.'"

"I remember after the breakup of the Bell System, Charlie Brown [the new chairman] issued a declaration. It was something like, 'Our overarching goal is customer satisfaction.' Well, that just doesn't grab you like, 'Get every person who wants one a telephone.'"

"Back then, I think most people who worked at AT&T had a gen-uine, warm feeling for the company. You believed that you were doing good, not just for yourself but for the country. I don't think AT&T has had that for some time. Not to get too dramatic about it, but if there's a lack of calling, there's a lack of accountability too."

In retrospect, Tom can also see that for a number of years he was essen-tially a functioning alcoholic. "I never had an arrest or an accident.

There was no bottle in my desk drawer. What I did was just drink all the time. Like an IV drip."

Years later, Tom inspires deep feelings among his former colleagues and friends, who share a great admiration for his intelligence and a lingering frustration at the self-inflicted waste of his talents. "I know that God did not give me half of what He gave Tom," Achmad says. "For someone with that promise, it was also his responsibility to develop it."

During the sixty-day grace period that AT&T grants its downsized brethren, some of Tom's teammates managed to find other jobs within the company. A few took early retirement. Tom made a fitful effort to find another position even as his specialty, strategic planning, was contracting throughout the firm. "If I had looked harder, I might have been able to find something. I would have had to take a demotion."

His wife urged him to be more aggressive—to find some job, any job, within AT&T. She had a healthy imagination and anticipated that her husband (pushing fifty, and a fifteen-year company man) would have a tough time out on the street.

"I had six or seven months sustenance as part of my severance package," Tom says. "I thought I could afford . . ." His voice drifts off. "I misjudged the thing."

Within several months of his exit date, Tom sent out hundreds of resumes. There were a handful of interviews, but not one job offer.

As the months of unemployment wore on, in the fall and then through the winter of 1995, Tom grew more and more depressed. As his family had feared, he drank more and more, and with a desperate edge that was frightening. By this time, no one could describe him as a functioning alcoholic. Tom was beginning to fall apart.

He could be a nasty drunk, and his insults would sting. Not many people were spared. Tom would snap at friends and family, including his two younger daughters. That fall, his two sisters broached the subject of his drinking with him.

Remarkably, it was the first time anyone in his family had directly confronted Tom. This was part of a quietly entrenched family pattern of denial. Howard's brother was an alcoholic who was forced to undergo a liver transplant; both Anne and Alison's first husbands were alcoholics. But for many years, the word was never spoken. In one typical scene, Ross, Alison's first husband, appeared totally drunk at his in-laws' house for a family dinner. He politely said hello, passed out on a bed, and did not reappear until the next morning. "Everyone pretended that he was just really tired," Alison laughs. "It's classic. Everybody colludes to deny the truth. That's what happened with Tom."

In the wake of the layoff, as Tom's drinking worsened, Anne came to feel that the time had come for extreme action, perhaps even an orchestrated intervention.

First, she and Alison approached Tom with the gentlest of overtures. They told him his drinking was out of control and was affecting his kids. Wasn't it time to get some help?

"What you say is so," was Tom's stilted reply. But for the next six months, he kept on drinking.

Anne and Alison both tried to get their father to confront Tom, thinking that perhaps his voice would be heard. But Howard could not begin to acknowledge his son's condition.

Finally, the sisters decided that there was no alternative to the ordeal of a family intervention. Alison talked to Elizabeth, Tom's wife, and she agreed. Anne suggested the Hazelden clinic, and Howard offered to help foot the bill.

A professional counselor flew to Alison's house the night before for a dress rehearsal with the nine people who would attend the next morning: five of Tom's friends from AT&T, as well as his wife, father, and two sisters.

Prepare a written statement, the counselor told them, elaborating on these three sentences:

I see your alcoholism affecting me in these ways.

I see your alcoholism affecting you in these ways.

This is what will happen if you continue to drink.

Tom was supposed to arrive the next morning at nine o'clock, but he was early, so Alison, knowing what lay ahead, had to endure forty-five minutes of small talk with her brother. They sat at her long kitchen table, staring out at the woods that surround her house, and chatted idly about woodchucks. Then everyone walked in the door.

The Hazelden counselor approached Tom. "I'm Brian. We're here to talk to you." Tom immediately understood what was happening.

Gathered around the kitchen table, his friends and family began to speak, one by one. His old friend Bobby talked about how he and Tom had drifted apart. Their daughters had become close when the two families were spending Sunday afternoons together, but the visits had stopped when Bobby felt uncomfortable exposing his daughter to Tom's drinking.

Another friend, Rana, described how he had relied on Tom's emotional support to help him through his own personal troubles. Rana told Tom that if he continued to drink, he would lose a friend.

Anne's statement was a model of controlled anger. She was very upset at the way Tom had treated people she loved. Alison described how she and her sister had had to bear the brunt of coping with their mother's final illness. Tom's drinking made him useless then, she said. Maybe alcohol helped destroy his first marriage, she added.

Many people were in tears, but Tom was dry-eyed, opaque. No one could guess how he would ultimately respond.

Elizabeth spoke last. She read a letter that her father, himself a recovering alcoholic, had written to his son-in-law. "You never make me laugh anymore," Elizabeth told her husband. She admitted that she herself had not acknowledged the truth of his addiction. "I've been playing along with you for a long time, but I'm not going to do it anymore," she said.

The counselor took his cue.

"You've heard these people speak," he said to Tom. His voice was flat, but he looked directly at Tom and there was an urgency in his eyes. "Will you do something about this now?"

Yes, Tom said softly. Everyone jumped up from the table. The relief was enormous, almost palpable.

"It really was a wrenching experience," Tom says. "My only alternative was to get a change of clothes, throw them in the back of the car, and disappear." Tom could contemplate such drastic action, but he could never take it. He drove with Brian to the airport.

"It's a beautiful day in Minnesota, what can I say?" Tom said with a laugh when he was midway through his twenty-eight-day treatment. "This is thirty years of drinking catching up with me, and I'm just grateful to God and my family for getting me here."

"There were no ballplayers or actors while I was at the clinic," Tom recalls, "but there were many out-of-work executives. One fellow was offered a job while he was at Hazelden, and the company wanted him to start immediately. There was a big debate about what this man should do. But a big part of overcoming alcoholism is being honest. So this guy screwed up his courage, called the president of the company, and explained the situation. It turned out that the president was himself a 1979 graduate of Hazelden. The guy said, 'Take all the time you need. The job will be waiting when you get out.'"

More naturally comfortable with Calvinism than the ideology of the twelve steps, Tom was not a quick convert to the Hazelden regimen. In the end, though, he found a way to make it his own.

"I'm not a cynic about it, because it's effective," Tom says. "Their insistence on the disease theory was hard for me to accept. My ambivalence is based on good old-fashioned Protestant self-reliance. You know, 'You're a bum, it's your own damn fault, so do something about it.' They say, 'You poor sick puppy, you need therapy. And what you might need is a kick in the pants.'"

But for Tom, Hazelden really was a kick in the pants. He left the clinic on his fiftieth birthday. To welcome Tom home, his daughters made banners and posters. There were presents, a homemade cake, and a real feeling of hope.

If life obeyed the conventions of poetic justice, the plot of Tom's life would here take a positive turn. He would find a good job, repair his battered marriage, live peacefully in the house he loves so much. But a year and a half after his return from Hazelden, he had no new job, his marriage had ended, and his house was about to be lost.

The final estrangement between Tom and his wife came during the seven months that they lived apart because Elizabeth had taken a new job. She and Tom agreed not to disrupt the children's school year: one of them would drive five hours each weekend so the girls could spend all of Saturday and Sunday with their mother. They would see where they stood at the end of the term.

For a while, Tom fantasized that the separation would help them find a way to come together, but he knew that was a distant hope. Instead, in their months apart, Elizabeth pulled further away. After a while, she and Tom were united only in fury and disappointment.

"I don't know if the marriage was any good anyway, but losing my job ended it, and put my kids and me in turmoil," Tom says. "This is a total and unredeemable disaster for my wife. She cannot understand it. She believes, perhaps rightly, that I did not do all that I could to avoid this disaster.

"My characteristic trait is that I believe things will turn out okay. So perhaps I don't do what I need to do to make sure that they do turn out okay."

At critical junctures, when he must choose a course—left or right, forward or back—Tom cannot move. Whether Elizabeth ever recognized or understood this essential quality in her husband, it certainly had never been tested before Tom lost his job, and he and his family had to face financial trouble for the first time.

In the first few months after he left AT&T—that golden interlude, the outplacement consultants say, when you stand your best chance of landing a new job—Elizabeth worried that Tom was not doing enough to find work. Tom was still drinking at this stage, and until he was sober, a job search would have been fruitless. Even after he returned from Hazelden, though, Elizabeth wondered if Tom was doing all he could to find work, or even all he said he was doing.

At some point, it seems clear, her compassion turned to anger. "She feels that I betrayed her," Tom says. "Her rational way of looking at it is that I let her down, badly. This wasn't part of the deal she thought she was getting when she married me."

Alison is naturally more sympathetic to her brother. "Elizabeth is a tough cookie, and I've always rather liked her. I think when she and Tom married she had expectations of a certain kind of life. That was the contract she thought she had. Now that it's fallen apart, she's just in a rage. And because she's a survivor, she's taking care of herself. There is no compassion, none." Howard adds, "For Elizabeth, you can't excuse failure, so you condemn it."

As so often happens, the couple's dream house became a symbol of their marriage. They had both fallen in love with the eighteenth-century house as soon as they saw it. It is a handsome, elegant Center Hall colonial, with four large, airy bedrooms. A huge stone fireplace, one of six in the house, anchors the living room. In the kitchen, large glass windows open onto a peaceful scene of trees and grass and sky. In 1992, less than two years before the AT&T downsizing, Tom and Elizabeth stretched their budget to buy the house and the five-acre property that surrounds it.

"We got married, and my wife and I both had certain expectations of what the future would bring," Tom says. "This house was at the pinnacle of her expectations. So when the contracts were drawn up to sell it—this was one of several deals that fell through before the bank foreclosed—it was like the gates slamming down.

"When the papers were signed, Elizabeth wept. I did, too. But not where anyone could see."

Inevitably, the tension and separation between Tom and Elizabeth took a toll on their daughters. They are lovely, spirited, bright girls. "I'm proud of them," Tom says. "They do things well and with enthusiasm." Amity plays the saxophone and the guitar; Abigail is an aspiring writer grappling, at that moment, with the inexplicably difficult subject of sixth-grade boys.

"About 95 percent of the time, Abigail is bubbly, and then there'll be some words or a sulk," Tom said during the months he spent alone with the girls. "Most of the time I don't even know what it's about. On the other hand, I guess there are things she feels she doesn't want to discuss with me, and Mom's not around and I don't understand. And of course I don't understand, because I don't have the faintest idea what's going on!"

he laughs. "That will last for a day or two. Her mother's not here, so it must be my fault. And it's my fault that she isn't here. That's hard."

"With Amity, the thing that will reduce her to tears is when Abigail and I have sharp words. She'll literally clap her hands over her ears and run. There's already enough disruption, she doesn't want any more.

"Amity has this intense desire to go to Arizona," Tom says, the aftereffect of a school social studies project. He would love nothing more than to take her. As he imagines the journey, Tom sounds as if he is yearning once again for the freedom of his own youth, "when you could throw your possessions in the back of a Volkswagen and just take off.

"Ideally we'd find someone around here who has a motor home who would rent it out on the sly. We could just mosey—we might not even make Arizona, it doesn't matter. But Amity and I, we could just wander where your fancy takes you. Get in the car and head vaguely toward some destination. Interstates only when absolutely necessary. That's a pleasant thought."

After Tom's first marriage broke up, he saw his daughters less and less, partly because he got considerably behind in child support payments. It was years before these wounds began to heal. Only recently has Tom managed to repair the rift with his oldest daughter, Jessica. He is determined not to repeat this failure with his second family.

"This subject took up a lot of time with the preachers at Hazelden. Time and distance and money," says Tom. "I appear to have abandoned them, and I did not want to abandon them, but as far as anyone can see I did. . . . In Alcoholics Anonymous they emphasize that shame is a terrible emotion, and one of the paralyzing ones. And I guess I'm ashamed."

At Hazelden, Tom had remarked in one meeting that he did not even know if he had a grandchild, the relationship with his daughter Jessica was so strained. In fact, he did have an infant granddaughter at that moment. When the baby was almost a year old, Jessica called to tell her father the news and to invite him to see her daughter. Tom took

Abigail and Amity and they drove up to Peterborough, New Hampshire, where Jessica lives.

"The baby is delightful. But it was an edgy visit, and we were both a little on guard. It wasn't a long visit because we were both wanting it so much to be good, and it was."

Over the years there had been less strain between Tom and his second-eldest daughter, Tory, now twenty-three. Recently, though, their relationship became more troubled. Still, Tom says, "Tory is capable and resilient. She's always ranked about 225th on my list of worries."

As it became clear that a second divorce was unavoidable, Tom savored his final months with his daughters. They gave him a reason to get out of bed in the morning, to be sober when they stepped off the school bus in the afternoon.

"The kids are both his anchor and his excuse, an excuse not to do what he needs to do for himself," says Alison.

As the final separation drew near, Tom dreaded the day. Over the July 4th weekend, he and Elizabeth had agreed, Tom would pack up his van and drive his daughters away.

In the two and a half years since he left AT&T, Tom has had two interludes of real work. For four months, he worked part time as a consultant to a small local business publication, a family-owned start-up hoping to increase its revenues and profits. Tom's mandate, essentially, was to offer the owners the benefit of his judgment and imagination, along with the financial expertise he acquired working with small business customers of AT&T.

He made several valuable recommendations, arranging for a new accounting firm that would better track the firm's cash flow and setting up a system to improve its accounts receivable. Tom also proposed a long-term growth strategy, but the owners chose not to pursue it.

The assignment did not evolve into a full-time job, as Tom thought it might, but it temporarily lifted his spirits. The job also suggested to Tom that he could make a plausible career for himself as an independent consultant to small businesses: "I know a little bit about a lot and I know where to find somebody who knows a lot about a lot, usually for free. I'm a fixer. Just in the nearest two counties, there are ten or fifteen firms I might try."

He admits that he has not been aggressive about seeking out that work, though, and it would be pointless to ask why. Paralysis is not rational, after all.

A second episode of work appeared through a family connection; a relative of Alison's husband was a successful young entrepreneur who owned a boat shop. It was a small operation, with just a handful of employees. Tom was hired as a counterman who would also offer consulting advice. The position was far beneath his abilities, and the pay was minimal, but it was a start. After a very long time, Tom was walking back into the working world.

It was unclear what went wrong, exactly. The owner followed several of Tom's substantive suggestions for the business, but perhaps he felt that Tom was not handling the office drudgery as efficiently as he should have. Tom had commented once that he thought the owner should be better conserving his cash flow—successful small businessmen often get into trouble when they rack up several million in revenues, spend too much on capital investments, and suddenly face a liquidity crunch. Perhaps that remark was seen as an unwelcome intrusion.

For whatever reason, after he had been on the job for two months, Tom was suddenly fired. He hadn't seen it coming, and the shock made him snap. He drove home, quickly downed a couple of drinks, and called Alison. She watched the liquor take effect as she sat with her brother at his kitchen table. "He was really thrown. I think it felt like total rejection for reasons he didn't understand." After a while, Alison insisted that they go outside to take a walk. They got Tom's black Labrador retriever, Lady, and tramped along a country road for about an hour.

For the next several days Tom kept on drinking, but the prospect of returning to alcoholic oblivion seemed too awful. He told himself that he simply must stop, and he did. Still, Tom's hold on sobriety is fragile, and he knows it.

A few months after this setback, Tom received more distressing news. Ross, Alison's ex-husband and a longtime alcoholic, had died an ugly death of liver failure at the age of fifty-six. Ross and Alison had split up in 1981, but Tom had sustained a friendship with his former brother-in-law—a connection that began, in fact, when the two young men would go out drinking together in local bars.

Tom saw the obvious and bleak parallels between Ross's life story and his own. Ross had lost his job as an executive at American Express in the mid 1980s, when his division was disbanded. After that, he floundered. He remarried and started a second family, launched a small business that never quite took off, racked up substantial debts, divorced again, and supported himself in part with money from his parents. All the while he drank, until his liver was finally destroyed. In his final weeks, Ross refused to see a doctor until it was too late to postpone his death. "When I get out of the hospital, my life is going to be totally different," he told his children a few days before he died.

Tom had silenced many voices over the years, but this warning he did hear: *When your time is up, it's up.*

When Tom was first divorced and out of work, he lived on a boat until AT&T hired him and he rejoined the professional classes. He was in his early thirties then; now he is past fifty. If he gives up now, it might be for good.

Tom feels a conflict within himself, "a clash between basic optimism and increasing paralysis. It's hard to be optimistic when you feel that lifting a finger is too painful." At times, he can summon a genuine, childlike enthusiasm for all the lovely delights that life can bring. "The first crocus and the start of spring training means the world will be all right," he tells himself one icy winter morning. At that moment, he believes it.

"There are times when one can't see any conceivable way out, and it feels like it will just never, ever end. But maybe things are going into a new phase. I feel a bit like I did when I was nineteen or twenty, living on an Indian reservation. What exquisite joy it was to pack up all your worldly goods in the back of a Volkswagen and take off. You could go from disaster to disaster, but you could still go.

"I still have a naive optimism that life is not all salt mines and striving. There's more—there should be, there can be.

"You know the story of the ant and the grasshopper? The ant is digging and digging to prepare for winter. The grasshopper is doing nothing. And finally winter comes. Where's the grasshopper? In a roadster, heading for Florida, he runs over the ant. Maybe there's a roadster lurking somewhere in my future."

On most days, paralysis proves the stronger force. "I've been thinking about this," Tom says, "and for some reason I've been withdrawing more and more. Even the things I like to do, I don't do. I didn't plant a garden this year, and I can't remember the last time that happened. I guess it's classical depression setting in." His isolation deepens. "I see people rarely—only real estate agents and bill collectors. I am awfully lonely."

When his dog got sick, Tom realized how dependent he had become on its companionship. "The dog was just leaning on me at every possible moment. Well, I realized, that's what I always feel like doing when I'm sick. Then one day she couldn't pick herself up to get out of the car." A vet diagnosed a raging case of Lyme disease.

"This is what this hermetic living has done. You get preternaturally attached to any life force. I have to go someplace to rejoin the human race.

"Look," he says, momentarily distracting himself, "there's a robin chasing a blue jay. The blue jay must be trying to steal one of its eggs."

There is, in Tom, both a profound despair and a beautiful love of life. Who can say which will ultimately prevail?

When the bank foreclosed on his house, Tom thought about moving to New Hampshire to live near his children. He has sworn not to abandon them, and that resolve is a rare positive force in his life.

Though his wife filed a tough divorce suit, the holiday season brought a sign that the family might find some peace. Elizabeth invited her estranged husband for Thanksgiving dinner, and Tom prepared his traditional tartar sauce, served every year with shrimp. "Pickles, onion, black olives and mayonnaise," he explains, "a little of this and a little of that until it looks right."

If Tom does move to New Hampshire, however, the well-intended gesture could prove self-defeating. "If he goes, he has to pull himself together," says Alison, with a rare note of exasperation. "He can't just sit in a one-room cabin. I can understand the impulse, but if he lives as a derelict, what's the point?"

It is a gloomy fact of adolescence, Alison adds, that teenagers run away from parents who make them feel ashamed. "Part of the problem is that when Tom looks scraggly, he looks really scraggly. He won't shave, he'll let his hair grow out. Adolescents don't want to be seen with their parents in the first place, and I'm not sure Tom understands that." Anne agrees. "Tom is an adoring father," she says, "but he has never raised an adolescent. He could be setting himself up for heartbreak."

At thirteen, Abigail is sullen and silent around her father. Her rejection pains Tom, though he believes that Abigail knows he adores her. Amity, three years younger, feels divided by the divorce. In a secret box with sliding levers, she stores a lucky charm, made out of a smashed penny, that she and her father took with them from a recent trip to a science museum. Tom keeps his in his pocket, and it is with him wherever he goes.

His father's financial support has helped sustain Tom through his many months of unemployment. He looks for work, but fitfully. For a few days a week he drives a limo, occasionally ferrying executives to Newark Airport.

He has become used to a solitary life of occasional, semi-menial work. On some level, Tom may feel that no job is better than a job that is far beneath his abilities. He is caught with his own conflicts, Alison feels, "his own attitudes toward what is acceptable work." Better to be driving a limo, which is so obviously inappropriate, than to choose a different kind of compromise. "But at this point," Alison says, "anything is better than nothing."

"I haven't counted Tom out," says Anne in a pained voice. "But I do despair for him."

"When you adopt invisibility as a cloak, you have to wear it," Howard says. "I shudder at what may become of Tom. Here's all this brilliance and charm and ability and it's being siphoned off by the world around us, and by Tom himself.

"I have a profound affection and love for my son, but also a queer gene which means I sometimes have to be realistic. That's a very uncomfortable gene to have, by the way. I, too, am a fundamental optimist, but I've been willing to bust some skulls to achieve it. But Tom has always had this bemused attitude toward everything and everyone around him, as if he were up in the clouds, observing the scurrying ants down below.

"There is such a vast difference between us. I don't extol the difference, but Tom never cooked up batches of vanilla extract in his basement and sold them door to door under the name Utility Products Company, as I did when I was thirteen. There's been none of that for Tom.

"What is usually called success would have been so easy for Tom, and he knew it. That's why he was contemptuous of it." Does Howard himself feel contempt for his son? "Contempt and sorrow. I have contempt for anyone who has it in him to do anything he wants, and doesn't." A moment later, Howard regrets his harsh words. "Tom has this boundless love. . . ."

———————

When Alison contemplates the arc of Tom's life, she sees a sad continuum: "Not having it come together." She pauses for a moment, and connects the thought: "Not *making* it come together?

"He is a loving man, and I'd like to see him find some peace. At heart I am an optimist, but things don't always get better. I don't feel hopeless about Tom, yet I'm not hopeful either.

"You want him to have an epiphany and wake up one day transformed. It doesn't happen that way. Nobody can rescue Tom. He can only rescue himself."

For the moment, though, Tom is frozen. His past identity as a company man seems as distant as a dream; his present reality feels too desolate to comprehend.

When Tom came home from the hospital, a nine-year-old boy who had survived the polio that ravaged so many lives, he walked into his house and began to climb the stairs. He took three steps, collapsed, and started to cry. It was so painful to pick himself up.

It still is.

CONCLUSION

They made separate journeys, none of them simple or untroubled. Patterns and themes emerge from these life stories, but there are no tidy endings. How could there be? None of us lead tidy lives.

These six people worked at AT&T long enough so that the company began to take on the characteristics of a family. They shared a largely inarticulated sense that the organization was a coherent and even caring entity that made considered judgments which could be anticipated and understood. But unforeseen events occurred.

Laboring mostly in the middle layers of AT&T's bureaucracy, these people were buffeted by the random forces of corporate decision-making. Along with many of their colleagues, they were simply in the wrong department when the downsizing began. Yet, when the company severed its ties with them, the experience challenged their basic beliefs.

In any defining life episode, people unwittingly repeat long-entrenched patterns of behavior, so this experience galvanized some and left others debilitated and bereft. Larry found strength in his early fame. Barbara was sustained by a resolute self-sufficiency. Kyle revived the productive spirit of his rebellious youth. Maggie held on to a feisty, native optimism. Vince and Tom, two sons of powerful and successful fathers, confronted the most difficult of family legacies. Though their personal histories are quite different, they both experienced a certain drift in their lives for a long time after they were laid off.

———————

Several years after they were downsized, where are these six men and women? Five of the six—everyone but Tom—have held on to new corporate jobs. By the simplest measures of worldly success they are doing well. They make more money than they did at AT&T. Their social status has not suffered. When a neighbor asks, "What do you do?" they feel comfortable with the answer they have to give.

They need to feel some stability in their working lives, even as they recognize that any sense of constancy must be as contingent as the contemporary American workplace—always vulnerable to shifts in technology, new product cycles, the inevitable management shuffles. As a group, they still face the everyday pressures and paradoxes of corporate life.

Vince, having weathered a changing of the guard in his new company's executive suite, has found that the shift does not jeopardize his position. Asked to take a lateral transfer to another department, he said yes without hesitation: He goes where they tell him to go.

Larry is kept busy by the wireless boom. His company can't hire employees fast enough, and he is constantly interviewing hopeful young engineers. They are fellow techies and Larry respects them, but he understands that they belong to a very different generation. Today's twenty-five-year-old engineers have no dream of beginning and ending their careers on the New Jersey campus of Bell Labs.

Barbara spends much of her time on the road, shuttling between her company's headquarters and the various outposts of the conglomerate that is her main client. As she navigates its bureaucracy, she is well served by her newfound pragmatism and flexibility. "I accept the fact that everything is in a state of flux," she says.

Kyle, at NCR, worked first as a consultant at AT&T. For all the chaos and upheaval at the headquarters in Basking Ridge, Kyle was struck by how the essential reality of the bureaucracy did not change: The hierarchy endures. When his bosses asked him to leave AT&T to work on several new accounts, Kyle was grateful for the reprieve.

Maggie keeps her sense of humor as she negotiates the new systems and procedures put in place after the Bell Atlantic–Nynex merger. Part of an army of ex-operators fighting the battle for market share in the telecommunications industry, she has no emotion invested in the outcome. Her eye is squarely on her paycheck.

Tom works in a plant nursery not far from his old house. The job makes little use of his mind but, Tom has found, physical labor can be its own reward. His love of plants and flowers, nurtured in his mother's garden, sustains him. "This is a business whose only purpose is beauty," Tom says. "No one needs another freesia, but if it gives you pleasure, you should have it."

Emerging from the shadow of their loss, these men and women have been forced to reconsider the meaning of work in their lives. For all of them it was a process of scaling back, of dismantling earlier-established expectations that work would bring them personal validation.

Shedding prior assumptions, these six people now neither hope nor expect to move up the corporate ladder. Where their careers once conformed to clearly staged, linear paths—the ladder was there, and it could be climbed—they now proceed along a more staggered track. For all of us in corporate America, the bond between company and employee has become a more nebulous connection, something that shifts according to circumstances.

This new reality will likely endure in good economic times and in bad. As the U.S. expansion moved into 1998, with the unemployment rate approaching a 25-year low and new job growth accelerating, companies still continued to restructure and downsize. As a result, a lingering sense of insecurity among employees produced only modest pressure for wage increases. (That is one reason, economists argue, that inflation has been kept in check.)

At the same time, many companies found themselves fighting to attract and retain their most valuable employees. Small wonder, given the legacy of past downsizing and the creep of contingent-work arrangements: on-call workers, part-timers, independent contractors.

This understanding has been internalized by today's company men and women. Those whose skills are in demand are more likely to leave one organization for another, while their less marketable colleagues feel vulnerable to forces beyond their control.

Surely the old social contract, that basic exchange of loyalty for security, has been destroyed. Nothing definite has yet taken its place, but there are early signs of what may emerge. The relationship will be tenuous and contingent. The organization's need for flexibility, in both its workforce and in its production processes, will surely prevail and inspire in its employees an intensified individualism. Some people will find the energy and resiliency to pursue their self-interest in this changing environment; emotional detachment will serve them well. For others, this process will be more arduous.

How will an organization encourage its employees to respect its long-term interests and serve the purpose of the firm? Without such a commitment, can any business truly prosper? There are no easy answers to these questions. The marketplace has never been a benevolent universe, of course, but a harsher self-interest—of all parties—has now started to form within it.

Some business theorists envision a new workplace that will accommodate both organizational flexibility and individual fulfillment. In their hopeful vision, companies will offer opportunities; employees will provide labor and talent. Workers will shuttle between projects and employers while organizations add and subtract staffers in a seamless ebb and flow.

Can we allow ourselves any such optimism? If the experiences of these six people are any indication, this process will be messy, and the concomitant dislocation severe. "I must manage my own career" is indeed the brave new rallying cry of today's company man, but it must be tempered by one basic fact: Power, as ever, resides with the organization.

NOTES

Overview

page 2.   History of job security relies on Sanford Jacoby, *Employing Bureaucracy* (New York: Columbia University Press, 1985).

page 3.   Fortune 500 statistics from *Fortune* magazine.

page 7.   Growth of contingent work force: For example, a 1997 study by economist Susan Houseman at the W. E. Upjohn Institute for Employment Research reports widespread "flexible staffing arrangements" among a sample of 550 companies: 72 percent of firms use part-time workers; 38 percent use short-term hires; 44 percent use independent contract workers.

page 10.   Displaced Workers Survey data from Bureau of Labor Statistics; Jennifer M. Gardner, "Worker Displacement: A Decade of Change," *BLS Bulletin*, July 1995; interviews with economists Steve Hipple and Jay Meisenheimer.

page 11.   "Since it is possible": Henry Farber, "The Changing Face of Job Loss in the United States, 1981–1995," Working Paper, Princeton University, May 1997, p. 7.

page 13.   By the 1990s, because more women were employed (and fewer of them left their jobs): see Alison J. Wellington, "Changes in the Male/Female Wage Gap," *Journal of Human Resources*, 28, no. 2: 383–411. 1993.

AT&T

page 51.   Section on Alexander Graham Bell relies on Robert V. Bruce, *Bell: Alexander Graham Bell and the Conquest of Solitude* (Ithaca: Cornell University Press, 1973).

page 52.   "What we wanted to do": Vail quoted in Leonard Schlesinger, *Chronicles of Corporate Change* (Lexington, MA: Lexington Books, 1987), p. 6.

page 52.   By 1902, 1500 firms: Schlesinger, p. 7.

page 57.   "It was a natural monopoly": Judge Harold Greene quoted in Steve Coll, *The Deal of the Century* (New York: Atheneum, 1986), p. 358.

page 61.   "I told Bob Allen": Quoted in L. J. Davis, "When AT&T Plays Hardball," *New York Times Magazine*, June 9, 1991, p. 32.

page 61.   The difference between the first and the final offer: *Fortune*, June 17, 1991, p. 127.

BIBLIOGRAPHY

Abraham, Katharine G. "Restructuring the Employment Relationship: The Growth of Market-Mediated Work Arrangements." In *New Developments in the Labor Market,* Katharine Abraham and Robert McKersie, eds. Cambridge: MIT Press, 1990.

Argyle, Michael. *The Psychology of Social Class.* London: Routledge, 1994.

Arlen, Michael J. *Thirty Seconds.* New York: Farrar, Straus, Giroux, 1980.

Bennett, Amanda. *The Death of the Organization Man.* New York: William Morrow, 1990.

Blackwell, Trevor, and Jeremy Seabrook. *Talking Work: An Oral History.* London: Faber and Faber, 1996.

Bridges, William. *Job Shift: How to Prosper in a Workplace Without Jobs.* Reading, MA: Addison-Wesley, 1994.

Brooks, John. *Telephone: The First Hundred Years.* New York: Harper & Row, 1976.

Bruce, Robert V. *Alexander Graham Bell and the Conquest of Solitude.* Ithaca, NY: Cornell University Press, 1973.

Business Week. "Rethinking Work." Oct. 17, 1994.

Cameron, Kim S., Sarah J. Freeman, and Aneil K. Mishra. "Downsizing and Redesigning Organizations," in *Organizational Change and Redesign,* George P. Huber and William H. Glick, eds. New York: Oxford University Press, 1993.

Cappelli, Peter, et al., editors. *Change at Work.* New York: Oxford University Press, 1997.

Cappelli, Peter. "Rethinking Employment," prepared for the British Journal of Industrial Relations Conference, May 29–31, 1995.

Cassidy, John. "All Worked Up." *New Yorker,* April 22, 1996.

Coll, Steve. *The Deal of the Century: The Breakup of AT&T.* New York: Atheneum, 1986.

Diebold, Francis X., David Neumark, and Daniel Polsky. "Job Stability in the United States." National Bureau of Economic Research, Working Paper 4859, September 1994.

Drucker, Peter. *Managing in a Time of Great Change.* New York: Truman Talley Books/Dutton, 1995.

———. *Post Capitalist Society.* New York: Harper Business, 1993.

Ehrenreich. Barbara. *Fear of Falling: The Inner Life of the Middle* Class. New York: Pantheon, 1989.

Farber, Henry S. "Are Lifetime Jobs Disappearing? Job Duration in the United States: 1973–1993. Working Paper #341. Industrial Relations Section. Princeton University. January 1995.

———. "The Changing Face of Job Loss in the United States, 1981–1995." Princeton University, May 1997.

———. "The Incidence and Costs of Job Loss: 1982–1991." Brookings Institution Paper, 1993.

Feather, Norman T. *The Psychological Impact of Unemployment*. New York: Springer-Verlag, 1990.

Gardner, Jennifer M. "Worker Displacement: a decade of change" *Bureau of Labor Statistics Bulletin*, July 1995.

Gordon, David M. *Fat and Mean: The Corporate Squeeze of Working Americans and the Myth of Managerial "Downsizing."* New York: Martin Kessler Books/Free Press, 1996.

Harrison, Bennett. *Lean and Mean: The Changing Landscape of Corporate Power in the Age of Flexibility*. New York: Basic Books, 1994.

Handy, Charles B. *The Age of Unreason*. London: Business Books, 1989.

Heckscher, Charles. *White-Collar Blues: Management Loyalties in an Age of Corporate Restructuring*. New York: Basic Books, 1995.

Houck, John W., and Oliver F. Williams, eds. *Is the Good Corporation Dead?* Lanham, MD: Rowman & Littlefield, 1996.

Howard, Ann, ed. *The Changing Nature of Work*. San Francisco: Jossey-Bass, 1995.

Jacoby, Sanford. *Employing Bureaucracy: Managers, Unions and the Transformation of Work in American Industry, 1900–1945*. New York: Columbia University Press, 1985.

Jahoda, Marie. *Employment and Unemployment: A Social-Psychological Analysis*. Cambridge, England: Cambridge University Press, 1982.

Katz, Harry C., ed. *Telecommunications: Restructuring Work and Employment Relations Worldwide*. Ithaca, NY: Cornell University Press, 1997.

Keefe, Jeffrey, and Karen Boroff. "Telecommunications Labor-Management Relations: One Decade after the AT&T Divestiture," in *Contemporary Collective Bargaining in the Private Sector*, Paula B. Voos, ed. Madison, WI: Industrial Relations Research Association, 1994.

Keller, John. "AT&T's Robert Allen Gets Sharp Criticism Over Layoffs, Losses." *Wall Street Journal*, Feb. 22, 1996.

Lash, Scott, and John Urry. *The End of Organized Capitalism*. Cambridge, England: Polity Press, 1987.

Leinberger, Paul, and Bruce Tucker. *The New Individualists: The Generation After the Organization Man*. New York: HarperCollins, 1991.

Leventman, Paula Goldman. *Professionals Out of Work*. New York: Free Press, 1981.

Loomis, Carol. "AT&T Has No Clothes." *Fortune*, Feb. 5, 1996.

Marcotte, Dave E. "Has Job Stability Declined? Evidence from the Panel Study of Income Dynamics." Center for Governmental Studies, Northern Illinois University, February 1996.

Meyer, G. J. *Executive Blues: Down and Out in Corporate America.* New York: Franklin Square Press, 1995.

New York Times. The Downsizing of America. New York: Times Books, 1996.

Newman, Katherine S. *Declining Fortunes: The Withering of the American Dream.* New York: Basic Books, 1993.

———. *Falling from Grace: The Experience of Downward Mobility in the American Middle Class.* New York: Free Press, 1988.

Nocera, Joseph. "Living with Layoffs." *Fortune,* April 1, 1996, pp. 69–71.

Noer, David. *Healing the Wounds: Overcoming the Trauma of Layoffs and Revitalizing the Downsized Organization.* San Francisco: Jossey-Bass, 1993.

O'Reilly, Brian. "Ma Bell's Orphans." *Fortune,* April 1, 1996, pp. 88–96.

Osterman, Paul. *Employment Futures: Reorganization, Dislocation and Public Policy.* New York: Oxford University Press, 1988.

———(ed.). *Broken Ladders: Managerial Careers in the New Economy.* New York: Oxford University Press, 1996.

Paige, Arthur W. *The Bell Telephone System.* New York: Harper & Brothers, 1941.

Piore, Michael J., and Charles F. Sabel. *The Second Industrial Divide: Possibilities for Prosperity.* New York: Basic Books, 1984.

Ransome, Paul. *Job Security and Social Stability: The Impact of Mass Unemployment on Expectations of Work.* Aldershot, England: Avebury, 1995.

———. *The Work Paradigm: A Theoretical Investigation of Concepts of Work.* Aldershot, England: Avebury, 1996.

Rifkin, Jeremy. *The End of Work: The Decline of the Global Labor Force and the Dawn of the Post-Market Era.* New York: G. P. Putnam, 1995.

Rose, Stephen J. "Declining Job Security and the Professionalization of Opportunity." National Commission for Employment Policy, Research Report No. 95-04, May 1995.

Russakoff, Dale, and Steven Pearlstein. "At AT&T, a Connection Broken." *Washington Post,* May 19, 1996.

Sampson, Anthony. *Company Man: The Rise and Fall of Corporate Life.* London: HarperCollins, 1995.

Samuelson, Robert J. *The Good Life and Its Discontents: the American Dream in the Age of Entitlement.* New York: Times Books, 1995.

Schlesinger, Leonard: *Chronicles of Corporate Change: Management Lessons from AT&T and Its Offspring.* Lexington, MA: Lexington Books, 1987.

Sennett, Richard, and Jonathan Cobb. *The Hidden Injuries of Class.* New York: Knopf, 1973.

Sloan, Allan. "For Whom the Bell Tolls." *Newsweek,* Jan. 15, 1996.

———. "The Hit Men." *Newsweek,* Feb. 26, 1996.

Swinnerton, Kenneth, and Wial, Howard. "Is Job Stability Declining in the U.S. Economy?" *Industrial and Labor Relations Review*, Vol. 48, No. 2, January 1995.

Terkel, Studs. *Working*. New York: Pantheon Books, 1972.

Time. "What Ever Happened to the Great American Job?" March 29, 1993.

Tomasko, Robert. *Downsizing: Reshaping the Corporation for the Future*. New York: Amacom, 1987.

U.S. Council of Economic Advisers. "Job Creation and Employment Opportunities: The United States Labor Market, 1993–1996." April 23, 1996.

U.S. Department of Labor. *Report on the American Workforce*. Washington, DC: GPO, 1995.

Useem, Michael. *Investor Capitalism: How Money Managers Are Changing the Face of Corporate America*. New York: Basic Books, 1996.

Warr, P. B. *Work, Unemployment and Mental Health*. Oxford, England: Clarendon Press, 1987.

Wolfe, Alan, ed. *America at Century's End*. Berkeley: University of California Press, 1991.

Wysocki, Bernard, Jr. "Retaining Employees Turns Into a Hot Topic." *Wall Street Journal*, September 8, 1997.

ACKNOWLEDGMENTS

My first debt is to the six men and women, as well as their families and friends, who welcomed me into their lives, with a special thanks to Tom Chase and his family.

Gloria Loomis, my agent, first believed in me as a writer, for which I am deeply grateful. I thank her for her support and wise counsel.

Janet Coleman at The Free Press conceived this project, championed its cause, and provided astute editorial guidance along the way. Elizabeth Maguire enthusiastically guided the manuscript to completion.

Emily Altman, Paul Brown, Sue Dawson, and Julie Rudolph read the manuscript in all its incarnations, and I thank them for their perceptive insights, constructive criticisms, and great friendship.

I benefited greatly from conversations with Richard Sennett at New York University, who generously read part of an early draft. Michael Kahan at Brooklyn College and Michael Useem at the Wharton School provided keen economic and political perspective. Thanks also to Glen Elder and Arne Kalleberg at the University of North Carolina, Claudia Goldin at Harvard University, Charles Heckscher at Rutgers University, Elizabeth Hegeman at John Jay College, and Sanford Jacoby and David Lewin at UCLA.

Jay Meisenheimer at the Bureau of Labor Statistics helped me navigate the statistical waters, cheerfully answering all my queries; thanks also to his colleagues Steve Hipple and Sharon Cohaney.

Among the consultants I interviewed, I thank the two John Challengers, Sr. and Jr., of Challenger, Gray and Christmas; Eric Greenberg of the American Management Asssociation; David Noer; David Opton of Exec-U-Net. Harry Levinson offered a useful psychological perspective.

John Moody read an early chapter draft and made very helpful suggestions. Melissa Jeffries was a very able research assistant.

Ed Block provided great insight into the history of a unique American institution. Thomas Chandy at UCLA offered his expertise on the early years of the Bell System.

AT&T spokesman Burke Stinson was as open and forthcoming as his job allowed, and I thank him for all the time and energy he devoted to this project. Jim Byrnes, Eileen Connolly, Mark Siegel, and Kelly Statmore (among others in the media department) provided facts and data, as did archivist Sheldon Hochheiser and human resources manager Andrea McGregor. At Lucent Technologies, I was assisted by Jane Moulton and Dick Muldoon; at NCR, by Bob Farkas and Betty Terrill.

Many anonymous employees of AT&T shared their thoughts and feelings about the company, and I thank them for their candor. Among the AT&T employees, past and present, whom I can thank by name are Zulfikar Ali, Randy Berridge, David Barnes, Glyn Bolar, David Burns, Bob Cain and his Pittsburgh troops, Janice Cooley, Doug Dunn, David Guay, Achmad Hassan, Chuck Levine, Ken Matinale, Jim Meadows, Rana Nanjappa, Gerry Nelson, Claire Powell, and Ken Whelan.

Thanks also to Matthew Adler, William Bridges, Janice Dunham, Kenneth Eisold, Bridget Flanagan, Jesse Jones, Margaret Jiuliano, Bob Shnayerson, Analyn Swan, and George Taber.

Thanks to my mother, who first introduced me to the world of books. My sister Diane offered emotional sustenance and a haven in a weekend office; my sister Julie was an unfailing source of encouragement. In writing this book, I relied upon the support and patience of my husband, Charles, and my daughter, Pamela; I am always grateful for their love. And my heartfelt thanks to Hazel Weinberg.

INDEX